VA Benefits - The Definitive Guide to Obtaining Your Benefits from the Department of Veterans Affairs

The Definitive Guide to Getting Your Benefits from the Department of Veterans Affairs.

Preface: This book is designed to help you get your compensation and pension benefits from the Department of Veterans Affairs. All links in this book are current as of the time of writing, and updates will be released when possible, however most resources can be found by visiting the Department of Veterans Affairs website.

The First Step: Preparation

Many people think that the first step begins with putting your application in for benefits through the VA. The first step, as with any endeavor however, is planning. The planning phase of your application is perhaps the most important step, because the planning stage is where you will gather and compile most of the information you will use to substantiate the claim for benefits and the medical nexus to your service. In the beginning of any claim for benefits, you have to remember that the VA doesn't know you, what has happened to you, or how your injuries affect your daily life, they will basically take the role of an insurance company who wants to ensure that they don't pay out any money for a situation that does not meet the requirements of law. The good news is that the law is published for public review, and this gives you the power to become informed. The best way to ensure that your story is told accurately and effectively is to obtain all the pertinent information ahead of time, especially with the normal backlog of VA claims. The VA will normally have anywhere from a four month to one year window on the completion of a claim, and that is if the claim is relatively straight forward and placed with the VA online. While the VA has a "duty to assist" you have to remember that this duty is only to assist in compiling the information that is required to complete a claim, not necessarily the information to approve a claim.

So the first few things to consider when starting to apply for benefits through the VA are, 1) Medical information 2) Effects of activities of daily living 3) Dates of injuries, duty stations, etc. and 4) Names of platoon members (if a death occurred for PTSD purposes). Perhaps the most important records will be your in service medical records, because they will show that an injury occurred while in service and a nexus to your service is absolutely necessary to receive benefits. The nexus clause that the VA uses states that any injury you have sustained or condition you are diagnosed with must in some way be either caused by or during your active service or aggravated by your service. This means that your in service medical records are crucial to your success in receiving benefits. Prior to leaving active service, you are offered a chance to retain a complete copy of your medical record, and if you are not, you have the right to go to your medical department, Battalion Aid Station or hospital and request a copy. There is also the possibility of signing up for an ebenefits account and then requesting that copies of all your service records be forwarded to you.

If you have been to a civilian doctor or hospital for anything that is related to your injuries or conditions after you ended your active service, it is important to get a copy of those records too, and this should include any emergency room visits you may have. You can choose to let the VA gather them for you, but there is a time penalty inherent in that. For example, you put in your claim, then time passes until they send you the forms to release to the VA your medical records which you now have to send back, then they have to send this form to your doctor who now has around four weeks to satisfy the request and mail the information back. This is all before a VA representative even has a chance to look at your claim. You must also remember that you should understand your medical records and know the terminology associated with any diagnosis you are given. The folks who review your information are NOT doctors, they are VA employees who review the information gathered by the doctors who see you during your compensation and pension examination and then try to fit the information they are given into the mold given to them by Title 38 of the Code of Federal Regulations.

The second thing to consider is what effect these illnesses or injuries may have on your activities of daily living. This is actually one of the more in depth pieces of the puzzle. Many injuries or conditions can effect the body in multiple ways, because your body is a complete system and like a watch, when a gear goes bad the overall operation of the watch

2

as a whole is now lessened. Two of the most important words you will be introduced to in the book are the medical terms "co-morbid" and "sequelae" which means secondary to. Co-morbid means an injury or condition that exists at the same time and is connected to another injury or condition. For example, a person who has anxiety and asthma. If the person developed asthma in service, but did not develop anxiety until later, that person may still be eligible to receive benefits for the anxiety disorder because asthma and affective disorders like anxiety are co-morbid. So, a back problem may also end up having an effect on your knees due to a change in posture or gait, and an arm injury might effect your neck and shoulder. When a condition is sequelae or secondary to another condition, it means that it is caused or aggravated by that condition. For example you may have a service-connected disorder that requires medication, this medication may have, as a side effect, a propensity to cause high blood pressure. If you then develop high blood pressure, it can be considered sequelae to the original disorder due to the medication you are prescribed.

An important note here is that the VA evaluates according to current disability. This means that even if a disease or condition is degenerative and will cause more sever problems later on in life, your disability percentage will be determined by your functional impairment at the time of your evaluation. Keep in mind that you may return to the VA at any time and request an increase in disability rating when the condition does worsen, however this will mean the requirement for a new claim each time you request an increase.

How these problems effect your activities of daily living is key to your percentage rating. The basic activities of daily living are:

- Bathing and showering (washing the body)
- Bowel and bladder management (recognizing the need to relieve oneself)
- Dressing
- Eating (including chewing and swallowing)
- Feeding (setting up food and bringing it to the mouth)
- Functional mobility (moving from one place to another while performing activities)
- Personal device care

- Personal hygiene and grooming (including brushing/combing/styling hair)
- Toilet hygiene (completing the act of urinating/defecating)

Added to these can be considered such things as building and sustaining relationships, interacting with others, ability to complete tasks, ability to remember, and ability to complete work tasks. How these activities are effected will determine where you fall in the VA's rating scale. This is an area where it is extremely important to be honest with the evaluator. You may be tempted to grin and bear the pain when you come to a certain degree of extension or a certain state of walking or movement. This is natural, especially when the injury has been around for a long time, your mind and body will begin to "normalize" the pain, however you need to resist the temptation to simply accept a lower standard of life and instead to inform the examiner of when and how the pain affects you.

The dates when these things happened, when you were stationed where you were stationed, combat, training exercises, etc are important because they will be checked for accuracy and truthfulness. If you say that you were in combat during a time where no combat operations were recorded or sanctioned, its much more difficult to get your benefits. This is not to say that it isn't possible, because there are ways that are provided for in the Code that the VA uses that will enable you to still qualify. For instance, the VA has a clause that states that as long as 51% of the evidence on file supports the veterans claim for benefits, then the VA must decide in favor of the claimant. This could be extremely important if your service records contain redacted documents or you have signed a non-disclosure clause due to classified operations.

It is extremely important that if you have multiple issues, and this is where knowing what co-morbid conditions may apply to your situation will come in handy, that you apply for all of them at one time. If you have, for example, high blood pressure due to anxiety or due to the medication you are taking for another condition and you wait to claim it, it will result in having to put in a new claim and the wait time will start over unless you claim everything at the same time. You also must remember that the majority of your claim with the VA is still kept in paper file form. This means that every time you have to go for an examination, your entire file will be transported from the VA Regional office attending to your claim, to the location where your evaluation will take place. So, if you put in one claim, then put in a second later on, if you get called to attend an evaluation on the second issue, any work that was being done on the first issue must stop while your file is transported from one location to another, then wait for you to undergo the evaluation and then for the evaluator to complete the report and send the entire file back.

Step Two: Know The Code

The Department of Veterans Affairs utilizes a few different federal and US codes to determine what percentage of disability to assign. One of the most important pieces of code to know is Title 38 of the Code of Federal Regulations. A free internet based copy of Title 38 CFR can be found at http://www.ecfr.gov/cgi-bin/text-idx?tpl=/ecfrbrowse/Title38/38tab_02.tpl or by simply conducting a Google search for Title 38 CFR. I recommend using the ECFR.gov version because it has not been passed through any filters and is in its real and pure form, plus the online version is updated as new information, rules, or regulations are added or removed. The link for the 0-17 Department of Veterans Affairs is where the information we will be dealing with is located. Of particular interest is section 4. Schedule for Rating Disabilities. In this section, you will find the actual piece by piece breakdown of how a disability effects a person and what rating they will receive. It is extremely important that you review the appropriate section of code. Many issues will be examined in different detail in more than one section of the code, so deciding which section is most applicable to your condition is going to provide you with the correct ammunition for your claim.

For example: A former Marine injured her arm during a training exercise. We would go to Title 38 CFR and go to the link for the Department of Veterans Affairs. Next we would browse section 4. Schedule for Rating Disabilities, and then to Sub part B. Disability Ratings. If the injury was ,say, a muscular injury, we would go to §4.71a   Schedule of ratings— musculoskeletal system. Say this injury stops our Marine from moving her arm any more than 22 degrees from her side. Going down to the Shoulder And Arm portion, we see that lack of movement to 25 degrees from the side could rate between 30 to 40% depending on severity. However, Section §4.73   Schedule of ratings—muscle injuries may also more closely approximate the injury that our Marine suffered and if that is the case, the VA will use the more descriptive and accurate description of the injury based on the medical facts.

Being familiar with Title 38 CFR is critical to knowing what you deserve as far as a rating decision. The above scenario is a good example of why. Knowing exactly what your injury is and how it is looked at by the VA could mean the difference between a 30% rating and a 40% rating. It also gives you a slight advantage. Remember that when they send you for a medical evaluation for VA benefits, they send you to a doctor who works for the VA. This means that, even if it is unintentional, a possible conflict of interest exists right off the bat. However, by taking this section of code to your personal physician, you can show them what the VA is specifically looking for and your physician can then write a report accordingly. Mostly the VA wants to ensure that they are not paying out benefits to someone who is just malingering or who knows how to work the code. They will work from the stand point that they are going to want to disprove before they prove that an injury is substantiated. Your personal physician however is working for you specifically, and it is important to help them understand what exactly you are looking to substantiate with their assistance.

A note on the difference between VA disability and Social Security Disability. Most doctors are usually faced with doing evaluations for SSA disability, which is either all or nothing. You are either fully and completely disabled with the Social Security Administration or you are not disabled at all. This is completely different from the disability given by the Department of Veterans Affairs, because they will rate based on percentage of disability, with the presumption of sound condition at the entry to service in mind. This means that your regular doctor will likely not understand what the VA is looking for as far as disability and will probably assume that its all or nothing like SSA. This is why, if you intend on enlisting your civilian doctor to assist in providing evidence for your claim, that you should bring the applicable section of Title 38 CFR with you, so that they can evaluate you with an eye to what the VA requires as far as functional impairments are concerned. That having been said, it is also important to note that you can apply for social security disability and VA disability if the VA finds you to be 100% or if you are rated Permanently and Totally Disabled due to Individual Unemployability in an extra scheduler rating.

Title 38 of the US Code also covers some important items as far as disabilities are concerned. For example, 38 U.S. Code § 1132 - Presumption of sound condition states that anyone entered into the armed forces will be considered to have been in sound condition at the time of examination barring any defects found during said examination. That means that if you come out in any condition other than the "sound" condition you went in as, then you probably deserve compensation according to the schedule of rating disabilities. Most of the codes, Title 38 and 38 USC are no exception, contain fields for searching specific terms, so you don't have to worry about the necessity of pouring through each and every section of the code to find your particular situation or condition.

A note on honesty. It should go without saying that you should be honest in seeking benefits from the Department of Veterans Affairs. This does however go both ways. In the first, be honest about what you are claiming because you can and will be prosecuted for falsely claiming benefits from the VA, not to mention the fact that such a thing would be morally bankrupt. On the other hand, don't do the "military" thing and try to suck it up and say nothing. By being honest about the severity of your conditions or injuries, you are going to ensure that you receive the appropriate amount of compensation, but also the appropriate level of care. Once you reach certain levels of disability percentage, you rate medical care and pharmaceutical benefits through the VA, and with medication prices, that can be a huge benefit if you have maintenance medication or medication that is absolutely vital to your ability to live your everyday life.

Beginning the Application

As stated above, ensure that you already have all of the pertinent information that is going to be required, such as dates of active and reserve service, dates of deployments, dates of injuries and conditions, any type of medication you take and dosages, dates of hospitalizations, names and addresses of medical offices who have seen you for the claimed injuries or conditions, and applicable diagnosis made by medical professionals who have seen you.

Applications for compensation and pension benefits can be done by paper, but that will cause transit time to be an issue. Always remember that any paper based communication between you and the VA is going to include mail time, and then must be scanned into the VA database by VA personnel, which can include additional time depending on the current backlog. The best way of beginning your application is to us the Veterans Online Application or VONAPP located at http://vabenefits.vba.va.gov/vonapp/main.asp. This is the online version of the application and will directly communicate your information to the VA system, greatly reducing wait time. The application itself is relatively self explanatory and easy to use, so time will not be spent going through the individual steps of the application.

One thing that is of extreme importance is the VA form 21-4138, the Statement in Support of Claim. This document can be printed off and should be used by any person who has had contact with you and seen how your conditions or injuries affect your daily life, such as spouses, co-workers, family and friends. Again, honesty should be stressed in this, because their personal information will be required and contact could be initiated by the VA, also falsifying a claim is a federal offense and definitely not worth the risk. That having been said, often times a third party will be more honest than you will be about the impact of your disabilities, and these statements can be instrumental to the success of your claim.

By the completion of your application, you will be given the address of your regional VA benefits office. If you forget or lose the address, you can visit http://www2.va.gov/directory/guide/division_flsh.asp?dnum=3&isFlash=1 which will give you the option to choose your state and find the regional benefits office. This is where you will send all of the information you have gathered to support your claim. There are two other ways of sending information, other than via US Mail, that may help facilitate your documents being viewed faster. The first way is to sign up for an ebenefits account by going to www.ebenefits.va.gov you will need to present yourself to a VA facility to verify your identity in order to qualify for a premium account. This will enable you to scan your documents into your computer and electronically send them to the VA. Another resource to use is the network of

8

VSO's (Veterans Services Organizations). These folks are usually involved in veterans organizations such as the DAV (Disabled American Veterans), VFW (Veterans of Foreign Wars), Marine Corp League and so on. A list of VSO's can be found at http://www1.va.gov/vso/ .

I recommend finding a VSO who has an officer on site at the regional office where your benefits application will be reviewed. This way you could be able to email your documents to the VSO representative who you are working with and they can in turn hand that information directly to the VA office themselves. In order to start a relationship with a VSO, you will need to fill out a power of attorney VA Form 21-22. You do not have to be a member of the VSO's organizations, but it is recommended that you become a member of at least one to help continue the free representative services that they offer, and for the other veteran-based benefits that they offer, and advocate for with our legislative branch. Remember, the more people they have behind them, the harder it is to ignore their voice.

After the Application

After the application is put in, and you've sent in all your statements in support of claim and medical evidence, prepare to wait. Normal backlog for claims is anywhere between 4 to 12 months. During that time you will almost certainly be sent for a medical evaluation through a VA doctor, usually at a VA facility, unless none are available in your area, then they will contract out. At your evaluation, ensure that you are honest about your injuries and conditions and any pain thresholds you have regarding movement and body usage. It is highly recommended that a few days after your medical evaluation, you return to your closest VA facility and request a copy of the evaluation. This will show you whether the VA examiner listed all of your complaints, skipped over any pertinent information, lowered or raised the level of severity of any issues, or all around was honest in the evaluation process. This way, if there is a discrepancy between what you said and what they wrote, you can attempt to address it before the rating decision is made and possibly avoid the hassle of an appeal.

There is the possibility that your decision will come back unfavorable to you in some way. It could be the complaints listed, it could be that they deny a medical nexus, or it could be the percentage of disability that you are assigned. You have one year from the date the VA sends you its original decision notice to file what is called a Notice of Disagreement. This is the one thing that does not have a specific format for it. You should, however, remember the following points: 1. The Notice of Disagreement (NOD) should clearly show the words "Notice of Disagreement" along the top. 2. Your first and last name and VA File number (usually your social security number) along the top as well. I recommend using the header space in your word processor to ensure that your name and file number appear on the top of EVERY page. 3. The NOD must clearly state which parts of the VA decision you specifically disagree with. If you don't agree with the percentage rating, you should not only state that you don't agree with it, but why you don't agree with it and what percentage rating you feel that you deserve. This again is where Title 38 of the CFR is invaluable, along with the copy you retained of the VA evaluation. You should search specifically for what is called a "Clear and Unmistakable Error". Any information you told the evaluator and wasn't included, any information that was played down or not accurately reported, or any obvious mistakes would be considered a clear and unmistakable error. For example: One veteran was diagnosed with a Chronic strain of the mid-thoracic spine with minimal scoliosis and given a 20% rating. It was stated that a higher rating was not warranted because the examiner found no scoliosis. The diagnosis was with minimal scoliosis, showing that a clear and unmistakable error was made in the rating decision and a new decision was issued and backdated to when the original claim was entered.

Another point on the NOD is whether or not you are willing to accept review by a Decision Review Officer or DRO. This person is on staff at the VA regional office where your benefits application is processed and specifically reviews claims where a NOD has been filed. It can sometimes be beneficial for a DRO review, because sending your disagreement to the Board of Veterans Appeals will also have a wait time associated with it. If you are honest and in the right on your disabilities, and can back up your assertion with the appropriate code and medical evidence, a DRO review can often times shorten the wait you would otherwise have had to deal with going through the BVA (Board of Veterans Appeals).

For the most part, physical injuries are relatively straight forward. Painful motion, which is covered in Title 38 of the CFR is harder to pin down, but the section that describes it shows what the VA is willing to consider in rating for it. Psychological issues are much more difficult to pinpoint because of their nature. You must be acutely aware of the impact that your conditions have and it is recommended that you research the conditions and their effects. Google Scholar is an irreplaceable resource for medical information. This is where the term "co-morbid" will come in most handy, because that is the term used by medical professionals in their medical papers to describe conditions that exist together. Google Scholar will provide you with PDF versions, where available, which you can print out, review, and send to the VA as evidence in support of your claim.

Psychological Problems

With any continual injury or condition where your daily life has been impacted negatively in some way, you are bound to have some sort of depression. Depression and other affective disorders are more problematic than physical disabilities to pin down because they don't leave physically identifiable injuries. They may have physical symptoms, but the causes and the mechanisms by which they operate are often hidden or aren't well understood. With psychological problems, you should know a few things directly off the bat. The application you should put in for is for an Acquired Psychiatric Disorder to Include PTSD, this covers the gamut of psychiatric disorders and makes this application an application for any mental disorder if they do not diagnose with PTSD. This will keep you from having to file another claim for a different disability.

With these types of disabilities, you should be as educated as possible about how it came about and what residual effects they have on your body as a system. Here is a real world example: A former Marine was misdiagnosed with Reactive Airway Disease, when he should have been diagnosed with asthma. He was placed back on full duty and made to continue physical training. The constant lack of breath and fear of death and injury this caused ended up manifesting in Generalized Anxiety Disorder. When at the VA examination, he was told no link existed between asthma and anxiety, however a simple Google Scholar search for anxiety and co-morbid affective disorders yielded no fewer then seven published medical papers showing a link between exactly these two conditions. One study was even done on former military members who served during the Vietnam war era! During another examination, he was told that "no one ever died from asthma" yet a search on the Center for Disease Control's (CDC) website showed that over 2,000 people every year died as a direct result of asthma, and several more with asthma as a contributing factor.

The anxiety this Marine dealt with also contributed to high blood pressure and irritable bowel syndrome. IBS was granted as secondary because, not only did the condition itself contribute to IBS, but the medication used to assist in controlling the anxiety and co-morbid depression also caused bowel problems. Some of the medicine this Marine had to take also caused stomach problems and were erosive of the stomach and esophagus lining, which contributed to his having severe esophagitis. All of these conditions were combined and compensated because they were connected to the conditions that developed during service – anxiety and depression due to being made to PT with asthma. When this Marine came out of service, he was service connected for asthma at 10% and nothing else, after learning the techniques in this book, he is now at 100% Permanent and Total Disability due to Individual Unemployability.

An important resource to consider is the DSM or Diagnostic and Statistical Manual. This manual, whose title is somewhat of a misnomer, is the manual that medical professionals use to diagnose mental disorders. There are some resources that can be found that contain parts of the DSM, but mostly these resources use outdated versions of the manual. As of this writing DSM IV is the most current issue. The manual itself is usually available for purchase, however, even using back dated material can provide information on your specific disorder or condition.

The Board of Veterans Appeals

The Board of Veterans Appeals is a board of legal professionals employed by the VA to review decisions that have been disagreed with. This is an extremely important resource because veterans who have had similar disabilities and similar experiences will have been in the same position and will have already disputed the decisions on their claims. It is important to note that a BVA decision cannot be used as a precedent like your regular legal cases can be, HOWEVER, that being said – they can certainly demonstrate how the Board views the application of certain rules to a veteran's disability profile. For example: One veteran had an affective disorder and was given a GAF (Global Assessment of Functioning score – this is a score given to assess on a number scale how badly a particular psychiatric problem effects a veteran's daily life) of 30. This number means that the veteran had severe issues with normal function in daily life due to the disabilities he had from his psychological condition, going from 100 - Superior functioning in a wide range of activities, life's problems never seem to get out of hand, is sought out by others because of his or her many positive qualities. No symptoms, to a 1 - Persistent danger of severely hurting self or others (*e.g.*, recurrent violence) OR persistent inability to maintain minimal personal hygiene OR serious suicidal act with clear expectation of death (beyond this is Insufficient Information).

This veteran was given a percentage of disability for his psychiatric disorders of 50%, however by doing a simple search on the Board of Veterans Appeals website (search decisions) for GAF score of 30 in the exact words or phrase box and Generalized Anxiety Disorder in the top search box gives us (among other cases) Citation Nr: 1208930 Decision Date: 03/08/12   Archive Date: 03/19/12 DOCKET NO. 94-39 440 where a veteran was given a GAF score of 30 and was awarded a 70% disability rating and then for Total Disability due to Individual Unemployability. Not all situations will closely approximate your own, some veterans will have additional impairments or a different disability profile. It is critical that you put in the time to find the claims of the past that do most closely approximate your own.

Not only will the BVA decisions show you how the Board interprets and applies the law, but it will also provide you with cases that have been brought against the Department of Veterans Affairs and the rule of law that came from them. For example: if you are concerned about having an overwhelming pile of evidence in your favor and feel that what you have is adequate but perhaps not sufficient, you need only review Gilbert v. Derwinski, 1 Vet. App. 49, 53 (1990) to learn The United States Court of Appeals for Veterans Claims (the Court) stated that "a veteran need only demonstrate that there is an 'approximate balance of positive and negative evidence' in order to prevail." These cases will be peppered throughout the cases found on the Board of Veterans Appeals website, and special attention should be made to them.

Many of these cases exist where veterans have already taken issue with the rulings passed down from the VA, and have won, so use the work they have already gone through to substantiate your claim. Remember that you don't have to go through the DRO route and can simply go to the BVA as well. It's a gamble because you could go through a longer wait time either way, by requesting a DRO review and then having the decision come back unfavorable and going through the BVA anyway or by going through the BVA and having a longer wait when a DRO could have resolved the issue. This is where the VSO will represent you in the same fashion as what you might expect a lawyer to do. Thankfully, for those who are unable to make it to a BVA hearing in person, they allow for video conferencing at many VA facilities, so you and your representative can make your case "face to face" as it were.

Remember also that your congress person is a resource that can be used to express your discontent with your rating. There are two groups of persons to consider, the first is your state congress person. You can generally contact them via their website, but you will be required to fill out a form requesting assistance with your VA claim for legal purposes. Generally speaking they will not even consider dealing with you until this form is filled out, and to be clear, congressional intervention can increase your wait time in getting your claim completed. Another group of persons to consider is the group of congress persons on the Board of Veterans Affairs Oversight Committee. These lawmakers are specifically tasked with oversight of the operations of the Department of Veterans Affairs, and have much more pull in the greater scheme of things than your average congress person. I would recommend contacting your local congress person AND a member of the Committee because the Committee is a very busy group of people and may or may not be able to address your specific issue. Your local congress person will normally be directly invested in your happiness because you are a constituent and as a disabled veteran, have contact with veteran-based organizations, and can cause an issue for said congress person during the next election.

Additional Benefits

Once you hit 30% disability, you rate additional monies if you are married, have children, or take care of your parents (meaning that they are actually dependent on you for support). You will need to fill out VA Form 21-686c in order to add your dependents to the VA system and claim your additional benefits. Once your disabilities are service connected at 10% or more, you then qualify for VA medical care for those conditions, however at levels below 50% you will likely be required to pay a copay for your visits. If you end up being 100% or are below 100%, but have at least one service-connected disability ratable at 60 percent or more, OR two or more service-connected disabilities, at least one disability ratable at 40 percent or more with a combined rating of 70 percent or more, you may qualify for Total Disability due to Individual Unemployability. This is an extra scheduler rating, meaning that it can be granted beyond the rating schedule of disabilities in Title 38 of the CFR, if you are unable to maintain gainful employment due to your disabilities and is paid at the same amount as the 100% rating. It is extremely important that you remember that if you are TDIU, you cannot usually work and you must fill out a VA Form 21-4140 every year to certify that you have had no employment for the preceding year.

Many other benefits become available at the TDIU or 100% level. You may have commissary and exchange privileges, and your children may rate a stipend when they attend college. You will rate a military ID and your spouse will as well, plus you will rate a base decal to be able to go on base at any time. Your spouse will also be eligible for CHAMPVA medical benefits.

Keep in mind. All of this is if your TDIU is considered permanent. To find out, review your VA award letter and find the words, "This total disability is considered permanent" or "no further examinations are scheduled" or "Eligibility to dependents Chapter 35 DEA /

CHAMPVA" or similar. Otherwise, the rating is likely temporary and these benefits may not apply. Lastly, be aware that just because the VA calls your disability rating "permanent" or that they have no future examinations scheduled, DOES NOT MEAN that it is really permanent or that they will never subject you to an examination again! You must maintain the TDIU rating for 20 years for it to be protected against the VA subjecting you to another evaluation in an attempt to lower your disability percentage.

State Veterans Benefits

The following section contains a summary of some of the benefits offered by individual state Departments of Veterans Affairs. These benefits won't always translate into money in your pocket, but some of them can certainly save you money. For example, many states offer free or low cost hunting and fishing licenses for disabled vets, North Carolina only charges $10.00 for a lifetime license, and that can save you a significant amount of money if you are a hunter. All information included here is up to date as of the time of this writing, however, it should be considered a summary and you should review the individual state websites for a full and updated list of benefits.

Alabama State Veteran's Benefits

The state of Alabama provides several veteran benefits. This section offers a brief description of each of the following benefits.

- Housing Benefits
- Financial Assistance Benefits
- Employment Benefits
- Veterans Business Benefits
- Education Benefits
- Other State Veteran Benefits

Alabama Veteran Housing Programs
Alabama State Veterans Home Program
The State of Alabama is extending this special kind of care to veterans through a partnership

with the federal government and private industry. The Bill Nichols State Veterans Home in Alexander City has been "home" to hundreds of veterans since its opening in 1989. In January 1995, Alabama opened two more homes to veterans, the Floyd E. "Tut" Fann State Veterans Home in Huntsville, and the William F. Green State Veterans Home in Bay Minette.

Alabama Financial Assistance Programs

Ad Valorem Tax Exemptions
Homes of Totally Disabled Persons or Those Over Age 65:
Exemption is provided from ad valorem taxation of the home of any person who is totally disabled or who is 65 years of age or older, and who had a net annual income of $7,500.00 or less for income tax purposes for the last preceding year.

The home of any veteran which is or was acquired by him pursuant to the provisions of Public Law 702, 80th Congress (specially adapted housing grant) as amended by (38 USC) regardless of its value shall be exempt as long as the same is owned and occupied as a home by the veteran or his un-remarried widow.

Homes of Veterans/Widows Acquired Under Public Law 702:

Incompetent Veterans:
The property of all incompetent veterans to the value of $3,000.00 is exempt from ad valorem taxation.

Motor Vehicle Paid for by VA Grant:
Any disabled veteran of WW II or of any hostilities in which the United States was, is or shall be engaged against any foreign state who owns an automobile which has been, is or shall hereafter be all or partly paid for with funds furnished for such purposes by the U.S. Department of Veterans Affairs (VA), under the authority of any act of the Congress of the United States is entitled to exemptions from all license fees and ad valorem taxes on such motor vehicle provided the veteran keeps the vehicle only for private use.

Veterans Organizations:
All property owned by the American Legion or by Veterans of Foreign Wars or by the Disabled American Veterans, or any post thereof; provided, that such property is used and occupied exclusively by their organization.

Bonus for Southeast Asian War Prisoners
A gratuity in the amount of $500.00 shall be paid to any person who entered the armed services while a bona fide resident of the state of Alabama and who was imprisoned as a prisoner of war in North Vietnam, South Vietnam, Laos or Cambodia. If the person qualified for the payment of this bonus died while a prisoner, the gratuity shall be paid to the next of kin. All applications for bonus or gratuity payments must be made to the State Department of Veterans Affairs. No payment shall be made except on applications duly received and approved by the said agency.

Exemption of Debts Incurred Pursuant to National Housing Act or Veterans' Benefits
All debts or extensions of credit incurred pursuant to any provision of the act of Congress known as the National Housing Act, as the same now exists or may hereafter be amended or

supplemented, and all debts or extensions of credit incurred pursuant to any act of Congress relating to veterans' benefits, as the same now exists or may hereafter be amended or supplemented, are exempt from any law of this state relating to usury or prescribing or limiting interest rates.

Military Retiree Income Tax Exemption
Effective January 1, 1989, and for all successive tax years, all retirement or compensation received as retirement benefits by any person retired from the military service of the United States of America and survivor benefits derived therefrom is hereby exempt from any state, county or municipal income tax or like tax whatever name called.

Unemployment Compensation
A person who served in the armed forces of the United States and who is unemployed may be entitled to unemployment compensation based on their honorable military or naval service. Contact the nearest State Employment Compensation Claims Office. Pension or disability payments provided by the United States to the individuals who have completed the period of military service may disqualify such individual from receiving unemployment compensation.

Military Combat Pay Income Tax Exemption
Money paid by the United States to a person as compensation for active service as a member of the armed forces of the United States in a combat zone designed by executive order of the President of the United States shall not be subject to income taxes levied by the State of Alabama for the calendar year 1965 or any subsequent year.

Alabama Veteran Employment Programs

Job Status and Reemployment Rights
County and municipal officials who enter the military or naval service at a time when a state of national emergency has been declared to exist by the President of the United States, have preservation of job status and reemployment rights.

Any teacher entering the military service of the United States, who is not on continuing service status but who has accumulated one or more years of teaching experience immediately prior to entering military service, shall be given credit for such experience if such teacher is re-imposed within one year after release from military service.

Preference in State Classified Employment
All persons who have been honorably discharged from the United States armed forces at any time shall have five points added to any earned ratings in examination for entrance to the state classified service. Those honorably discharged veterans with the present existence of a service-connected disability and entitled to pension, compensation or disability allowance under existing laws shall have 10 points added to any earned ratings. Wives and widows of certain disabled or deceased veterans may have the 10 point preference extended to them and added to any earned ratings.

Membership in State Employees'/Teachers' Retirement System
Retirement benefits rights of state employees and teachers who enter the armed forces and

return to state employment after discharge are preserved. A member who enter the armed services and does not withdraw contributions, and who returns to said employment within one year after being honorably discharged, may be granted credit for military service up to four years, provided the employee pays an amount equal to four percent of the average compensation paid to a state employee during each claimed year of full-time military service, plus and together there with eight percent interest compounded from the last date of such claimed military service. The contributions must be made within a period of time equal to the length of service in the armed forces or before attainment of age 60, or in the case of a state policeman, age 56, whichever occurs first. No credit for military service shall be granted if such member is receiving military service retirement benefits.

Alabama Veterans Business Benefits

Business and Occupation License Exemptions for Disabled Veterans
Any bona fide permanent resident of Alabama who is a veteran of the Spanish American War, WW I, WW II or at any time past, present or future, when the United States was, is or shall be engaged in hostilities with any foreign state and who has physical disabilities of 25% or more whether service-connected or not, who conducts their business as a means of livelihood through their personal efforts and has no more than one employee and whose property (both real and personal) is valued at less than $5,000.00 and net income is less than $2,500.00 is entitled to businesses and occupations license exemptions of $25.00 for each state, county and municipality. There is not a deadline on these exemptions.

Business and Occupation License Exemptions for Veterans of WW II
Alabama veterans who served in the armed forces of the United States between September 16, 1940 and the termination of WW II or at any subsequent time when the United States was, is or shall be engaged in hostilities with any foreign state are entitled to exceptions on business of occupation license of $35.00 for each the state, county and municipality for a period, as to WW II veterans, or six years from July 24, 1953, or six years after date of discharge from military service, whichever is later. Post Korean veterans (Vietnam) have for a period of six years from January 1, 1964 until May 7, 1975, or six years after date of discharge, whichever is later. Such veterans whose property is valued at $7,000.00 or more, or whose net annual income is $3,000.00 or more, is limited to $15.00 exemptions from the state, county and municipality.

Forfeiture of Franchise
No corporate franchise shall be forfeited for non-use, if any of the managing officers of such corporation become engaged in military service of the United States and as a result thereof the corporation suspends operations, if the corporation has paid all its franchise and other taxes to the State.

Alabama Education Assistance Programs

G. I. Dependents' Scholarship Program
The Alabama Department of Veterans Affairs announces major changes to its Alabama G.I. Dependents' Scholarship program. This program provides free tuition, textbooks and instructional fees at any state-supported institution of higher learning, college or university to qualified dependents of eligible disabled veterans.

On March 18, 2014, Governor Robert Bentley signed into law Act No. 2014-177 that amended critical portions of the scholarship program. It eliminates the requirement that a veteran must have served during a wartime period or under extra-hazardous conditions.

Beginning in the fall 2014 semester, dependents of eligible peace-time veterans may now qualify to participate in the program if all other qualifications are met. Dependents previously denied education benefits based solely on the veterans' peace-time service dates must reapply by Aug. 1, 2015, to receive the full benefit.

Also beginning in the fall 2014 semester, the program will cover only undergraduate level courses at the in-state tuition rate. Students presently enrolled in the program will not have any change in their benefits.

Interested veterans, or their family members should visit their county veterans' service office for more information, or call 334-242-5077.Other Alabama State Veteran Benefits

Armed Forces Voter Registration and Absentee Voting

Members of the armed forces of the United States and their dependents may register and receive an absentee ballot for voting in the county of their Alabama permanent address by completing the federal postcard application form, "Federal Post Card Registration and Absentee Ballot Request" (Standard Form 76). This form may be obtained from the military unit's voting officer. The completed form should be mailed to the Board of Registrars in the county of his/her Alabama permanent address.

Commitment of Incompetent Veteran

Whenever it appears that an incompetent veteran of any war, military occupation or expedition is eligible for treatment in a U.S. Department of Veterans Affairs (VA) Medical Center is necessary for the proper care and treatment of such veteran, the courts of this state are hereby authorized to communicate with the administration with reference to available facilities and eligibility and, upon receipt of a certificate from the administration stating that there are facilities available in a VA Medical Center is entitled to hospitalization therein, the court may then direct such veteran's commitment to such hospital. Notice of such pending proceedings shall be furnished the person so committed, and his right to appear and defend shall not be denied.

Executive, Attestation and Acknowledgment Certification

Acknowledgments, proof of conveyance and affidavits may be taken by certain government, state or municipal officials or by any commissioned officer of any of the armed forces of the United States, within or outside the limits of the United States, and when such acknowledgment is taken by the latter, no seal of office is required and the signature of such commissioned officer is prima facie proof of his authority, and is retroactive as of December 7, 1941.

Fiduciaries in War Service

Any fiduciary engaged in war service may be removed from this office as such upon petition filed in the proper court having jurisdiction and again serve as such fiduciary at any time after the termination of their war service upon petition of the court.

Fishing License

Any person who is totally disabled and who has been a bona fide resident of this state for not

less than six months preceding the date of application may, upon the payment of a license fee of $1.00, procure a special annual fishing license. Guardianship for Veterans and Minor Dependents
The Uniform Veterans' Guardianship Act provides for the appointment of a guardian for veterans and their minor dependents who are mentally or physically incapacitated. This Act outlines the appointment process, duties, responsibilities, limits, taxing of costs and fees of guardianship. The control and accountability of the beneficiary's estate and income include only moneys received by the guardian from the U.S. Department of Veterans Affairs (VA) and all earnings, interest and profits derived.

Hunting License
No exemption is available for hunting license due to disability.

Military Leave of Absence
All officers and employees of the State of Alabama, or of any county, municipality, or other agency or political subdivision thereof, who shall be active members of the Alabama National Guard or naval militia, or of the Officers' Reserve Corps of the United States Army, or of the reserve components of the United Stated armed forces, shall be entitled to military or naval leave of absence from their respective civil duties and occupations on all days that they shall be engaged in field or coast defense or other training or on other service ordered under the provision of the below cited statute, or of the National Defense Act, or of the federal laws governing the United States reserves, without loss of pay, time, efficiency rating, annual vacation, or sick leave, but no such person granted such leave of absence with pay shall be paid for more than 21 working days at any one time.

Notice of Armed Forces Death
A written notice or communication from the Department of Defense, the Adjutant General of the Army, the Secretary of the Navy or other officer charged with the duty of sending such notice or communication to the effect that any person in the armed forces of our country, or serving as auxiliary thereto, is dead shall be accepted as evidence of the death of such person.

Official Report of Person Missing, Etc
An official written report or record or duly certified copy thereof, that a person is missing, missing in action, interned in a neutral country, or beleaguered, besieged or captured by an enemy or is dead or is alive, made by any officer or employee of the United States authorized by any law of the United States to make same, shall be received in any court, office or other place in this State as evidence as to the status of the person.

Peace Officers' Credit for Military Service
Any peace officer who becomes a member of the fund and who left employment and entered directly into the armed forces of the United States and who returned to work as a peace office within six months after release or discharge shall receive prior employment service credit for service in the military not to exceed five years.

Public Records
One copy of any public record (birth or marriage certificate, divorce decree, etc.) is furnished

free of charge when required by the U.S. Department of Veterans Affairs (VA) to be used in determining the eligibility of any person to participate in benefits made available by their federal agency.

Recording of Discharges
Honorable discharges and certificates of honorable service are recorded free of charge by probate judges.

Validation of Marriage of Divorced Persons
Marriages of all persons subsequent to a divorce decree granted in the State and not prohibiting the person from remarrying, are declared to be valid, notwithstanding that the decree of divorce did not specifically confer on such person the right to remarry. Many claims for pension and compensation against the U.S. Department of Veterans Affairs (VA) have been made effective by this law.

Wills
The will of a person, executed while in the armed forces, is admitted to probate when subscribing witness or witnesses are out of the state at the time the will is offered for probate; or when places of address of witnesses are unknown, upon oath of at least three persons that the signature to said will is in the handwriting of the person whose will it intends to be. Such will is acceptable when so proved.

Alaska State Veteran's Benefits

The state of Alaska provides several veteran benefits. This section offers a brief description of each of the following benefits.
Real Estate Benefits

- Employment Benefits
- Education Benefits
- Other State Veteran Benefits

Alaska Veteran Real Estate Benefits

Veterans Land Discount/Purchase Preference
The Veterans Land Discount program allows certain veterans to a 25 percent discount on the purchase price of state residential/recreational land. The discount may be used only once during the veteran's lifetime and may not be used in conjunction with the veterans preference.

Under the Veterans Land Sale Preference, before offering to the general public any unoccupied residential land by auction, a veteran has the exclusive opportunity purchase the land at a restricted sale at fair appraised market value. Parcels that are offered under this preference must be five acres or less, classified as settlement land and zoned for residential use only.

Property Tax Exemptions
Real property owned and occupied as the primary residence and permanent place of abode by a qualified disabled veteran whose disability was incurred or aggravated in the line of duty and whose disability has been rated as 50 percent or more by the military service or the U.S. Department of Veterans Affairs, is exempt from taxation on the first $150,000.00 of assessed valuation. Contact your local municipal tax assessor's office by March 15 for exemption for current year.

Veterans Housing and Residential Loans
The Alaska Housing Finance Corporation (AHFC) administers the Veterans Mortgage Program which offers financing for qualified veterans at lower interest rates. Active duty service in the Armed Forces, Public Health Service, NOAA or service as a cadet at the US Military, Air Force, Coast Guard or Naval Academy may qualify. Loans are generally processed rapidly, require little or no down payment, and often include lower interest.

AHFC also offers a Veterans Interest Rate Preference, in which a veteran receives a one percent lower interest rate on the first $30,000 of a bank loan when purchasing a new home, ask the bank handling the financing to implement this program for you. AHFC grants a preference to veterans for the rent or sale of a portion of its low cost housing projects units.

Alaska Veteran Employment Programs

Employment Preference Rights
Workplace Alaska in the Division of Personnel in the Department of Administration is the on-line recruitment process for all the states classified service positions. Every vacancy in the classified service, except those requiring registration with Job Service, are posted on the homepage and are available for on-line application. Vacancies are advertised in the Sunday editions of the Fairbanks News Miner, Juneau Empire, and Anchorage Daily News along with recruitment phone lines.

Veterans who possess the necessary qualifications for a given state job classification and served on active duty and received an honorable or general discharge during the dates listed on the employment application, are eligible for a state employment hiring preference.

Veterans Employment Services
The Veterans Services Section of the Employment Security Division of the Alaska Department of Labor and Workforce Development promotes employment, economic stability, and growth by operating a no-fee labor exchange that meets the needs of employers, job seekers, and veterans. The service provides job placement, job matching and referral, vocational counseling, and job search assistance.

Affirmative Action Plan
The State of Alaska 1998 Affirmative Action Plan affords all present and prospective state employees in the executive branch an equal opportunity for employment regardless of their

veteran‚s status - among many other factors.

The state will ensure there are no impermissible or artificial barriers for veterans or disabled veterans to cross in applying for state jobs, provide on-the-job training and assistance in locating qualified disabled applicants, recruit and employ qualified persons with disabilities and Vietnam era vets for state jobs, and sets up an informal complaint procedure. The plan is administered by the Office of Equal Employment Opportunity in the Division of Personnel.

Alaska Education Benefits

Free Tuition for Spouse or Dependent of Armed Services Member
The spouse or dependent of an armed services member who died in the line of duty or who died as a result of injuries sustained while in the line of duty or who was listed by the Department of Defense as a Prisoner of War or as Missing in Action is entitled to a waiver of undergraduate tuition and fees the students must be in good standing in a state supported educational institution in Alaska.

High School Diplomas
Operation Recognition, a nation-wide effort, recognizes that many World War II veterans went off to war and never returned to high school to get a diploma.

In Alaska, the Department of Education and Early Development may award diplomas to World War II vets living in Alaska, including Alaska Territorial Guard members, who served during the period of August 7, 1940 to July 5, 1947 and were honorably discharged or died in active service or were released from active duty because of a service-related disability. A family member may apply on behalf of a veteran who is deceased or incapacitated. Even ex-GIs with a Graduation Equivalency Diploma could apply.

Other Alaska State Veteran Benefits

Recording Veterans Report of Separation Form
A veteran may record, without fee, the original or a certified copy of his or her Armed Forces Report of Separation (DD-214 Form) at any State Recorder's office of the Department of Natural Resources.

The Recorder's office maintains 14 District offices throughout the state, overseeing 34 recording districts that record, index, and archive all of the documents that create the Official Public Record of the state of Alaska.

Disabled Veterans Parking Permits
Disabled Parking Permits are also obtained from the DMV, available to persons at least 50 percent disabled or medically handicapped, including persons disabled in the line of duty while serving in the Alaska Territorial Guard. Applicants must show reception of at least 50 percent disability compensation from a government agency or an affidavit signed by a physician licensed to practice in Alaska.

Veterans License Plates
Veterans License Plates, with the word 'veteran' and the symbol of each branch of service,

are available from the Division of Motor Vehicles upon submission of written proof of veterans status. Fee is $30 biennially. Purple Heart recipients and Alaska National Guard members may also purchase special plates for $30. Pearl Harbor Survivors and former POWs recipients may receive a special plate at no charge. A Disabled Veteran can register one vehicle without charge and receive a specially designed registration plate that displays recognition of the disabled veteran. With proof, persons disabled in the line of duty, who are 50 percent disabled or medically handicapped as a consequence of service are eligible. The plate does not display the standard handicap symbol and does not carry with it special parking privileges; however the standard wheelchair logo may be available depending upon the level of disability as described below.

Hunting and Fishing Licenses
Resident hunting and sport fishing licenses are available at no charge to honorably discharged veterans with a 50 percent or greater service-connected disability and Alaska residency. Applicants must have lived in Alaska for 12 consecutive months immediately preceding the application.

State Camping Pass
The legislature granted Disabled Alaskan Veterans (DAV) the right to receive one Alaska State Park Camping Pass free of charge. The DAV Camping Pass, which is valid in all developed Alaska State Park campgrounds, is good for two years.
To receive a free DAV camping pass, an eligible disabled veteran must present proof of a service connected disability and Alaska residency at either the Anchorage or Fairbanks DNR Public Information Centers (see below). Proof of residency can be in the form of an Alaskan Driver's License, Alaska Sport Fishing License, Alaska Voters Registration Card, or other documentation suitable to the department that proves Alaska residency.

Alaska Marine Highway Pass
A one-year pass on the ferries of the Alaska Marine Highway is available for veterans having a service-related disability. This pass entitles the disabled passenger and an attendant (if required by a physician) to travel at 50% of the regular passenger fare, between Alaska ports only, on all vessels, year-round.

Birthday Cards from the Governor
Birthday greetings from the Governor are available to veterans 80 years and older. Veterans or family or friends of veterans should contact the governor's office at least four weeks in advance and supply the name and address of the person to receive the card and appropriate proof of age.

Governor's Advocacy Award
Individuals who demonstrate an extraordinary personal concern, compassion, and commitment to veterans causes, veterans, and their families are eligible for the annual Governor's Veterans Advocacy Award. A winner could also have formed a new, innovative or creative volunteer program or project that benefits vets. Accomplishments must have been performed on a volunteer basis. Governor's Veterans Advocacy Award will be presented on Veterans Day, November 11th.

Military and Veterans Memorial Landmark Property
The Military and Veterans Landmark Property Program formally recognize memorials around the state built to honor the military and veterans of the armed forces. Information about the

memorials is important to understanding the sacrifices made by veterans in Alaska and America, the role of the military, and the history of our nation's wars.

Information about memorials will be preserved by the State of Alaska as an important part of its history. A record of each approved Landmark Property will be maintained by the Department of Military and Veterans Affairs, including a list of properties to be kept, to facilitate visitation to memorials for those interested in doing so. The state will provide an attractive, numbered certificate, suitable for framing, at no cost.

Wartime Letters - The Legacy Project
The Legacy Project is a unique and meaningful way to honor all veterans by preserving letters written by soldiers on the front and letters written to them from home.

A national, volunteer non-profit agency, known as The Legacy Project, began collecting letters from any American wartime period to preserves these treasured documents and therefore heighten appreciation of them.

Letters can be ones personally written or received, or written by a relative. These may include eyewitness accounts of battles or acts of heroism, encounters with famous military leaders, love letters, or any other irreplaceable messages or little-known stories that will offer historians and future generations a better understanding of those who served and sacrificed for country.

Military Credit Towards State Retirement
Certain members of the various state retirement programs may be eligible for additional credit for up to five years military service. Military service will increase your retirement service and monthly benefits. Although military service is not membership service, in certain cases it may count toward vesting and retirement eligibility. Visit site below, click on the retirement system of interest, scroll to Military Credit.

In the National Guard and Naval Militia Retirement System, anyone with at least 20 years of combined Alaska guard service, guard service in any other state, active military service and the reserves of them, of which at least 5 years must have been satisfactory service in any branch, may receive a small benefit upon separation from the Alaska army guard, air guard, or naval militia if you meet minimum eligibility provisions.

Arizona State Veteran's Benefits

The state of Arizona provides several veteran benefits. This section offers a brief description of each of the following benefits.

- Housing Benefits
- Financial Assistance Benefits
- Employment Benefits

- Education Benefits
- Other State Veteran Benefits

Arizona Veteran Housing Programs

Arizona State Veteran Home
The Arizona State Veteran Home is located in Phoenix at 4141 N. 3rd Street. It is a 200 bed, skilled care nursing facility operated and maintained by the Arizona Department of Veterans' Services. The Veteran Home offers different levels of nursing care and encourages residents to function at their highest level. The state of the - art facility has been designed to be both functional and provide a pleasing environment with a southwest atmosphere.

Visit the Arizona Department of Veterans Affairs website for contact information and benefits assistance.

Arizona Financial Assistance Benefits

Tax and License Fee Exemptions
1. To the extent not already excluded from Arizona gross income under set. 112 of the Internal Revenue Code, compensation received for active service as a member of the Armed Forces of the United States for any month during any part of which members served in a combat zone is exempt.

2. Federal (Civil Service or Military Retirement) payments up to $2,500.00 per year are exempt. NOTE: Contact the Arizona Department of Revenue (1-800-845-8192) for any veteran tax issues.

Property Tax: Exemption for property of widows, widowers, and disabled persons. A. The property of widows, widowers, and disabled persons who are residents of this state is exempt from taxation to the extent allowed by Article IX Â§ 2, 2.1, 2.2, and 2.3, Constitution of Arizona, and subject to the conditions and limitations prescribed by this section. NOTE: The exemption is applied to real estate first, then to a mobile home or an automobile. Contact your County Assessor office for eligibility.

Vehicle License Tax and Registration Fees
No license tax or registration fee shall be collected from any veteran for a personally owned vehicle if such veteran is certified by the U.S. Department of Veterans Affairs to be one hundred percent service-connected disabled and drawing compensation on that basis. A veteran residing in Arizona shall be exempt from a vehicle license tax on a vehicle acquired by the veteran through financial aid from the U.S. Department of Veterans Affairs.

Arizona Employment Benefits

Employment Preferences
Age Limit: An honorably discharged veteran shall be eligible for employment preference, rights, and privileges under any merit system in the state in the state or any political subdivision thereof, regardless of age, if otherwise qualified.

Civil Service: Veterans who pass an examination for employment by the state, county or city will have 5 points added to their certification score. The veteran must have served for more than six (6) months and be separated under honorable conditions. Veterans entitled to compensation for a service-connected disability will have 10 points added to their certification score. Certain spouses or surviving spouses shall be given a 5 point preference if the veteran died of a service-connected disability.

Fire Department: Members of any fire company inducted into the military establishment of the United States for military training are authorized reinstatement to their previous rating after discharge from military service.

Police And Fire Department: The period of military service shall be included in computing the length of service of the employee to determine eligibility for retirement.

Reserve Status/War Emergency: Appointive officers or employees of the state or of a political subdivision will be reinstated to their former position upon completion of military service to which (s) he was inducted or ordered during time of war or was called to service because of their status as an active or inactive member of the Reserves.

Arizona Education Benefits

Tuition and Fees-Deferred Payment
A veteran or eligible dependent who has applied for educational benefits under the G.I. Bill state-supported community colleges, colleges and universities may defer
payment of tuition, fees and required books for a period of 120 days with no interest charges. If, at the end of such period, the person has not received from the U.S. Department of Veterans Affairs the initial benefit monies for tuition and fees, an extension may be granted until such time benefits are received.

Visit the Arizona Department of Veterans Affairs website for contact information and benefits assistance.

Other Arizona State Veteran Benefits

Burial and Headstones
When a veteran or a surviving spouse dies without sufficient means for funeral expenses, the County Board of Supervisors is responsible to ensure that burial will not be in a portion of ground used exclusively for burial of paupers. A suitable plot will be used, and the county may apply to the U.S. Department of Veterans Affairs for expenses not to exceed $150.00.

When the county buries an indigent veteran, the county clerk will make an application to the U.S. Department of Veterans Affairs for a suitable headstone and make arrangements for it to be placed at the head of the grave.

Voting in Elections
Absentee registration and voting by active duty military personnel and their eligible dependents residing out of state may be accomplished by prior to 7:00 p.m. on an Election Day. The County recorder may accept a federal postcard application in lieu of an affidavit of registration.

Recording of Discharges
Any county recorder, free of charge shall record military discharge papers. Location of each

County Recorder's Office may be found in the blue pages of your area telephone directory.

Public Record Certification
Public officials shall issue without charge, certified copies of public records for use in making a claim for pension, compensation, allotment allowance, insurance, or other benefits from the United States.

Credit for Military Service for State Retirement Benefits
A participant of the state system or plan may receive credited past service or future service for active military service if the participant was honorably discharge from service. The period of military service for which the participant receives credited service is not on account with any other retirement system. Contact the nearest state personnel office for additional information and eligibility.

Hunting and Fishing Licenses
Resident hunting and fishing licenses for members of the armed forces on active duty, stationed in state are available upon application. Complimentary licenses may be granted to veteran's 70 years or older who have been residents of this state for 25 years. Complimentary licenses will be issued to veterans verified by the U.S. Department of Veterans Affairs to be one hundred percent service-connected disabled and who have been a resident for one year ore more. Note: Contact the nearest Department of Game and Fish office.

Arizona State Parks
The Arizona State Parks department announced from Fort Verde State Historic Park that the agency will be instituting a new program to provide Arizona's 100% permanently disabled veterans with a "Disabled Veterans Annual Day Use pass." The pass will provide qualified veterans with day use access to all twenty-seven State Parks.

Special License Plates
Medal of Honor: Any resident of Arizona who is a recipient of the Medal of Honor may apply for a distinctive number plate at no additional cost.

- Prisoner of War: Any resident of Arizona who is a former prisoner of war may apply for a distinctive number plate. An initial fee of $15.00 is charged in addition to the registration fee with an annual renewal fee of $5.00.

- Purple Heart: Any resident of Arizona who is a recipient of the Purple Heart may apply for a distinctive number plate. An initial fee of $25.00 is charged in addition to the registration fee with an annual renewal fee of $5.00.

- Pearl Harbor Survivors: Any resident of Arizona who was a member of the Armed Forces of the United States, received an honorable discharge, and was stationed at Pearl Harbor, the island of Oahu (or offshore not exceeding 3 miles), on December 7, 1941, during the hours of 7:55 A.M. to 9:45 A.M., is eligible for a Pearl Harbor distinctive number plate. An initial fee of $25.00 is charged in addition to the registration fee with an annual renewal fee of $5.00.

- National Guard: Any resident of Arizona who is or has been a member of the Arizona Air National Guard or Army National Guard may apply for a distinctive number plate. An initial and renewal fee of $25.00 is charged in addition to the registration fee.

- Veteran: Any resident of Arizona who was a member of the Armed Forces of the United

States and received an honorable discharge may apply for a distinctive number plate. An initial and renewal fee of $25.00 is charged in addition to the registration fee.

Transportation
Common carriers may give free or reduced rates to residents of homes for soldiers, and, with the consent of the Arizona Corporation Commission, to former soldiers and sailors for the purpose of attending any convention.

Arkansas State Veteran's Benefits

The state of Arkansas provides several veteran benefits. This section offers a brief description of each of the following benefits.

- Arkansas Veterans Home
- Financial Assistance Benefits
- Education Benefits
- Other State Veteran Benefits

Arkansas Veteran Housing Programs

Arkansas Veterans Home
Founded in Little Rock in 1980, as a domiciliary, the Arkansas Veterans Home now provides 55 domiciliary and 61 intermediate care nursing beds. The home provides a meaningful living environment for honorably discharged veterans. Residents also have full access to the U.S. Department of Veterans Affairs and Central Arkansas Veterans Healthcare System. With twenty-four hour nursing service and a staff physician, medical needs are fully met. With licensed social workers and an activities director, each resident has the support and encouragement he or she might need to promote a healthy active lifestyle.

Arkansas Financial Assistance Benefits

Personal Property Tax Exemption
Arkansas Veterans who have been rated, by the VA, as 100% service connected (Permanent and Total) or awarded Special Monthly Compensation for loss or loss of use of one or more limbs total blindness in one or both eyes are entitled to exemption of Homestead and Personal Property Tax. Widows, so long as they do not remarry, dependent children, during their minority, continue this entitlement. Widows, so long as they do not remarry, dependent children, during their minority, are also eligible for this entitlement if the veteran was killed or died in the scope of his military duties, is missing in action, or died from service connected causes as certified by the Veterans Administration.

Gross Receipt of Tax Exemption
or gross proceeds derived from the sale of motor vehicles and adaptive equipment to disabled veterans who have purchased the vehicles or equipment with the financial assistance of the

Veterans Administration as provided under 38 U.S.C. 1901-1905 (AR Code 26-52-401 (7) et. seq.) Gross receipts or proceeds derived from the sale of a new automobile to a veteran who is blind as a result of a service-connected injury. Registration will require an entitlement letter form the VA and will be limited to one new vehicle every two (2) years. This exemption defines automobile as a passenger vehicle or pick up truck but does not include trucks with a maximum goes load in excess of three-quarter (3/40 ton and does not include any trailer.

Income Tax Exemption
Provides an exemption of the first $6,000.00 of service pay or retired pay for members of the Armed Forces to include Reserve Components or for retired members who are residents of the State of Arkansas.

Arkansas Education Benefits

Educational Benefits
Arkansas Department of Higher Education (ADHE) has the authority to provide free tuition and fees at any state supported college, university, technical school, or vocational school; to the wife and children of any Arkansan who has been declared to be Prisoner of War or placed in a missing-in-action status since January 1, 1960. The same provisions apply to the surviving spouse and children of any Arkansas resident killed in action since 1960.

Other Arkansas State Veteran Benefits

Arkansas Department of Parks and Tourism
Arkansas resident veterans permanently service connected at a 100% disability rate may camp for half price in Arkansas State Parks. Proof of 100% status is required.

Arkansas Game and Fish Commission

Resident 3- year Disability Fishing License- RDC ($10.50) entitles all 100% totally and permanently disabled persons privileges of the Resident Sportsman's License (hunting) and the Resident Fisheries Conservation License (fishing). HIP registration is required to hunt game birds. To hunt waterfowl, state and federal waterfowl stamps are required in addition to HIP. A Trout permit must also be purchased to fish in certain waters. Certification will be accepted from Social Security, Veteran's Affairs or Railroad Retirement. Proof of one year's Arkansas residency is required to apply for this license. Valid for three years from date of purchase, recertification is required for renewal. These two licenses are only available from the Commission's Little Rock office. If you wish to purchase a license, bring proof of one year Arkansas residency, such as driver's licenses, state ID, property assessments, Arkansas state income tax forms and acceptable proof of disability.

License Plates
The Revenue Division will provide (upon receipt of proper certification letters) a number of special privileges and benefits for Arkansas residents, including special license plates for Congressional Medal of Honor recipients, Purple Heart recipients, Ex-Prisoners of War, Disabled Veterans, Pearl Harbor Survivors, Armed Forces Retired, and Military Reserve.

Arkansas State Veterans Cemetery
Dedicated in 2001, our cemetery is dedicated to providing an honorable place of rest for the veterans of the State of Arkansas. Our mission is to preserve the dignity, beauty and serenity of this cemetery to honor all who sacrificed to make possible the freedom that we are able to enjoy today.

California State Veteran's Benefits

The state of California provides several veteran benefits. This section offers a brief description of each of the following benefits.

- Housing Benefits
- Financial Assistance Benefits
- Employment Benefits
- Veteran Business Benefits
- Education Benefits
- Other State Veteran Benefits

California Veteran Housing Programs

Veterans Homes of California
The Benefits: Professional and low cost residential, assisted living and medical care facilities throughout California.

Who May Be Eligible: Aged or disabled U.S. veterans who are residents of California.

Calvet Farm and Home Loans
Direct loans from the State of California, highly competitive rates, quick processing, unbeatable earthquake and disaster coverage, and proven ability to work well with homeowner veterans.

Who May Be Eligible: Any veteran who served honorably on active duty in the Armed Forces of the United States, who resides in and wishes to purchase a farm or home in California.

Apply at any California Department of Veterans Affairs CalVet District Office (located in the state government section of your telephone book), or

California Department of Veterans Affairs
Farm and Home Loan Division
1227 'O' Street
Sacramento, CA 95814
1-800-952-5626

California Financial Assistance Benefits

Property Tax Exemptions
Property tax exemptions on the assessed value of a home of:

a) up to $111,296 if the total household income from all sources is over $49,979 per year.
b) up to $166,944 if the total household income from all sources is under $49,979 per year.

Who May Be Eligible: a) Wartime veterans who are in receipt of service-connected disability compensation at the totally disabled rate. b) Unmarried surviving spouses or registered domestic partners of veterans who are in receipt of service-connected death benefits. c) Wartime veterans who are service-connected for loss the use of two or more limbs. d) Wartime veterans who are service-connected for blindness.

To apply contact your local County Assessors Office (located in the county government section of your telephone book).

Motor Vehicle Registration Fees Waived
Waiver of registration fees and free license plates for one passenger motor vehicle, or one motorcycle, or one commercial motor vehicle of less than 8001 pounds unladen weight.

Who May Be Eligible: Medal of Honor recipients, American Ex-Prisoners of War and "disabled veterans" as defined in the "Disabled Veterans License Plate" section of this pamphlet.

California Employment Benefits

Employment and Unemployment Insurance Assistance
Assistance in obtaining training and employment as well assistance in obtaining unemployment insurance.

Who May Be Eligible: All veterans.

Veterans Preference in California Civil Service Examinations
Additional points added to the final score of a civil service examination as follows: a) Open Entrance Exams-15 points for a disabled veteran and 10 points for other veterans and surviving spouses. b) Open Non-promotional Entrance Exams-10 points for disabled veterans and 5 points for other veterans.

Who May Be Eligible: a) Veterans with service-connected disabilities rated at 10% or greater. b) "Wartime" veterans who served have served with honor. c) A veteran who served under honorable conditions for a period of at least 181 days d) Spouses of totally disabled service-connected veterans. e) Unmarried, surviving spouses of a veteran who has died of service-connected causes.

California Veteran Business Benefits

Business License, Tax and Fee Waiver
Waiver of municipal, county and state business license fees, taxes and fees, for veterans who hawk, peddle or vend any goods, wares or merchandise owned by the veteran, except

spirituous, malt, vinous or other intoxicating liquor, including sales from a fixed location.

Who May Be Eligible: Honorably discharged veterans who engage in sales (not services) activities may be eligible. Eligibility criteria differs based upon local jurisdiction.

Disabled Veteran Business Enterprise Opportunities
Certified veteran owned businesses can participate in the state goal of awarding 3% of all state contracts to disabled veterans through the Disabled Veteran Business Enterprise (DVBE) Program.

Who May Be Eligible: Veterans with a service-connected disability rated at 10% or greater who own at least 51% of a business, and who meet other eligibility criteria.

California Education Benefits

College Tuition Fee Waivers for Veterans' Dependents
Waiver of mandatory system-wide tuition and fees at any State of California Community College, California State University or University of California campus.

Who May Be Eligible: Plan A: The spouse, registered domestic partner, child (under the age of 27) or unmarried surviving spouse of a veteran who is totally service-connected disabled, or who has died of service-connected causes may qualify. Plan B: The child of a veteran who has a permanent service-connected disability. The child's income and value of support provided by a parent cannot exceed the national poverty level.

Non-Resident College Fee Waiver
Waiver of non-resident fees (pay at California resident rate) at all State of California Community Colleges, California State University or University of California campuses. Eligibility includes the following indiviuals:

- A student who is a veteran of the armed forces of the United States stationed in this state on active duty for more than one year immediately prior to being discharged from the armed forces is entitled to resident classification for the length of time he or she lives in this state after being discharged up to the minimum time necessary to become a resident.

- An undergraduate student who is a member of the Armed Forces of the United States stationed in this state on active duty, except a member of the Armed Forces assigned for educational purposes to a state-supported institution of higher education.

- An undergraduate student who is a natural or adopted child, stepchild, or spouse who is a dependent of a member of the armed forces of the United States stationed in this state on active duty.

- A student seeking a graduate degree who is a member of the Armed Forces of the United States stationed in this state on active duty, except a member of the Armed Forces assigned for educational purposes to a state-supported institution of higher education. There is a two-year limit for graduate level studies.

- A student seeking a graduate degree who is a natural or adopted child, stepchild, or spouse who is a dependent of a member of the armed forces of the United States stationed in this state on active duty. There is a one-year limit for graduate level studies.

Eligible students can apply at the Admissions Office of any California system campus.

Other California State Veteran Benefits

Disabled Veteran License Plates
Waiver of registration fees and free "DV" handicap parking license plates for one passenger motor vehicle, or one motorcycle, or one commercial motor vehicle of less than 8001 pounds unladen weight.

Who May Be Eligible: A "disabled veteran" is any person who, as a result of injury or disease suffered while on active service with the armed forces of the United States, suffers any of the following:

a) Has a disability which has been rated at 100 percent by the Department of Veterans Affairs or the military service from which the veteran was discharged, due to a diagnosed disease or disorder which substantially impairs or interferes with mobility or,

(b) Is so severely disabled as to be unable to move without the aid of an assistant device or,

(c) Has lost, or has lost use of, one or more limbs or,

(d) Has suffered permanent blindness, as defined in Section 19153 of the Welfare and Institutions Code.

Obtain a signed doctor's statement that indicates that the veteran in question has a service-connected disability with at least one of the above listed mobility impairments, complete DMV forms REG 195 and REG 256A, and mail the completed package to:

DMV PLACARD
P.O. Box 942869
Sacramento, CA 94269-0001
1-800-777-0133

Vehicle Registration Fee Waiver
Waiver of registration fees and free license plates for one passenger motor vehicle, or one motorcycle, or one commercial motor vehicle of less than 8001 pounds unladen weight.

Available to Medal of Honor recipients, American Ex-Prisoners of War and "disabled veterans" as defined in the "Disabled Veterans License Plate" section of this pamphlet.

Medal of Honor recipients should complete a DMV form REG 17A, and proof of receipt of the Medal of Honor. Ex-Prisoners of War should complete a DMV form REG 17, and proof of former status as a POW.

Applications and necessary documentation should be mailed to:

Department of Motor Vehicles
P.O. Box 932345
Sacramento, CA 94232
1-800-777-0133

www.dmv.ca.gov

Veterans Claims Representation
The Benefit: Professional, accredited, USDVA claims and ratings review, and representation in appellate processes.

Who May Be Eligible: Any veteran, dependent or veteran's survivor applying for USDVA benefits.

Fishing and Hunting Licenses
The Benefits: Reduced annual fees for fishing and hunting licenses.

Who May Be Eligible: Any veteran with a 50% or greater service-connected disability.

First time applicants must submit proof of their service-connected disability from the USDVA.

The California Department of Fish and Game
License and Revenue Branch
1740 N. Market Blvd.
Sacramento, CA 95834
Phone (916) 928-5805
Department of Fish & Wildlife/e

State of California Veterans Cemetery
The Benefit: Complete, professional burial services at no cost to veterans ($500 fee for spouses or dependents).

Who May Be Eligible: Veterans, dependents and survivors who meet USDVA eligibility requirements for burial in a national cemetery.

Veterans License Plates
These special California license plates may be ordered with the armed force or veterans service organization logo/emblem of your choice. Over 100 insignias are available, and your logo will be prominently displayed to the left of a six number/letter combination. Sequential plates are only $30 per year. You may also "personalize" your Vets Plates (your choice of up to 6 characters) for an additional one-time fee of $10.

The California Women Veterans Roster
Unfortunately, women veterans have not applied for or utilized their veterans benefits as have their male counterparts, which ultimately dilutes the voice of veterans overall. The California Women Veterans Roster is an information bridge that connects California's women veterans to the various resources and benefits available to them.

The roster is strictly confidential and used solely as a link among California's women veterans. Help give women the voice they earned through service to our country. If you are a woman veteran, join the California Women Veterans Roster! If you are not a woman veteran, please give the gift of information and pass a copy of the roster application form (see below) on to a woman veteran or someone you know associated with women veterans.

The California Veterans Registry at the California Veterans Memorial
The California Veterans Registry is a permanent record of all California Veterans -- past and

present -- who have served our nation since statehood was established in 1850. Whether cook or fighter pilot, mechanic or chief of staff, this memorial will honor them all, and forever immortalize the contributions that California veterans have made to their nation.

Each California veteran is entitled to the basic information of name, rank and branch of service. To create a truly living memorial, California veterans are encouraged to expand on the basic information by contributing to the enhanced registry.

Colorado State Veteran's Benefits

The state of Colorado provides several veteran benefits. This section offers a brief description of each of the following benefits.

- Housing Benefits
- Financial Assistance Benefits
- Employment Benefits
- Education Benefits
- Other State Veteran Benefits

Colorado Veteran Housing Programs

State Veterans' Home
Admission preference is given to Veterans, spouses, widows and mothers at State Veterans Center, Homelake, CO. With 40 operating beds in the domiciliary unit and 60 beds in nursing care service.

The Colorado State Veterans Nursing Home at Florence, CO with a bed capacity of 120 beds. Colorado State Veterans Nursing Home at Rifle, CO with a capacity of 100 beds. Colorado State Veterans Nursing Home at Walsenburg with a capacity of 120 beds. We have a new State Veterans Home. It is the Fitzimons State Veterans Home, located in Denver, CO. It has a capacity of 180 beds.

Colorado Financial Assistance Benefits

Colorado State Tax Advantage
SCR06-001 has passed and will be on the November ballot. It provides a Property Tax Exemption for 100% SC disabled veterans.

Retired Military Pay: Members of the Armed Forces can exclude up to $20,000 in any one taxable year from their retirement pay.

Eligibility: U.S. Armed Forces Retiree over 55 years or older.

Military Disability Retired Pay: Disability Portion - Length of Service Pay; Member on September 24, 1975 - No tax; Not Member on September 24, 1975 - Taxed, unless combat incurred. Retired Pay - Based solely on disability: Member on September 24, 1975 - No tax; Not Member on September 24, 1975 - Taxed, unless all pay based on disability and disability resulted from armed conflict, extra-hazardous service, simulated war, or an instrumentality of war.

VA Disability Dependency and Indemnity Compensation: Not subject to federal or state taxes.

Motor Vehicle Tax: No fee shall be charged to certain disabled Veterans or Ex-POWs who have established their right to benefits under public laws. Applies to subsequent vehicles, but only one at a time.

Burial Allowance
County allowance of up to $50 for burial and up to $50 for setting markers for pauper Veterans.

Colorado Veteran Employment Benefits

Employment Assistance
State Active Duty employee receives 15 days of paid military leave per year.

Eligibility: Colorado National Guard

Employment Preference
Disabled Veterans shall have 10 points added to their grades and non-disabled Veterans shall be credited with an additional 5 points for "state employment". For city and county governments that have a "Merit System" in place.

Colorado Veteran Education Benefits

Tuition Assistance
Any member of the Colorado National Guard is eligible for state tuition assistance, up to 100% tuition paid at any CO state-funded school depending on funding available. State funding can be used in conjunction with Federal Tuition Assistance. Deadline for Spring Semester is Dec. 1. Deadline for Fall Semester is July 1. Summer deadline is May 1 (if funding is available).

Eligibility: Colorado National Guard member must serve 2 years for each year granted.

Tuition Assistance for Children of POWs, MIAs, or Disabled/Deceased ARNG
Free tuition in certain State-support schools for children of prisoners of war or persons missing in actions who were Colorado residents when they entered the Armed Forces, or for children of Colorado National Guardsmen who died or were permanently disabled while on State active duty limited to dependents who do not qualify for Federal Education benefits.

Operation Recognition
Operation Recognition is a program to award High School diplomas to deserving and qualified

WWII, Korea and Vietnam Era Veterans. Operation Recognition, is authorized by Colorado State Law and is offered by the Colorado Board of Veterans Affairs in cooperation with the Colorado Department of Education and the Colorado Association of School Boards.

Other Colorado State Veteran Benefits

Special Vehicle License Plates
The State provides plates at no cost to the Veteran include: recipients of the Medal of Honor, recipients of the Purple Heart, to certain disabled wartime Veterans, special disabled (50% +)Veterans license plates, and special license plates for former POWs. Plates for honorably discharged Veterans may be purchased for nominal fee. January 2007, There will be issued a "Valor Plate" for those veterans who have received the Distinguished Service Cross, Navy Cross, Air Force DSC, and Survivors of Pearl Harbor and/or their surviving spouse.

Medical Benefits
Dental coverage and full medical for line-of-duty
Eligibility: Colorado National Guard

Hunting and Fishing Privileges
Fishing license: No fee for
Eligibility: 1) Member of the Armed Forces stationed as a resident patient at a military hospital or convalescent station, 2) any resident patient at a USDVA hospital located within the State, 3) any Veteran who is permanently and totally disabled.

Small Game Hunting and Fishing License: Free lifetime combination small-game hunting and fishing license.

Eligibility: Resident Veteran with a service-connected disability of 60% or more.

Connecticut State Veteran's Benefits

The state of Connecticut provides several veteran benefits. This section offers a brief description of each of the following benefits.

- Housing Benefits
- Financial Assistance Benefits
- Employment Benefits
- Education Benefits
- Other State Veteran Benefits

Connecticut Veteran Housing Programs

Connecticut Veterans' Home

39

The Department has a health care center with a capacity of 250 beds, a 50-bed substance abuse recovery program and a 500-bed Residential Program. Professional services are provided by staff physicians, Advanced Practice Registered Nurses, OT, PT, RT, dieticians and social workers are augmented by community specialists, as well as, networking to local VA and major area hospitals when appropriate. By Statute, veterans who are able to pay in whole or in part for programs or services determined by the applicable fee schedule will receive a monthly bill for such services rendered.

State Income Tax Excemptions

Connecticut veterans receiving federally taxable military retirement pay are eligible for an exemption from the state income tax. Connecticut applies a 50 percent exemption from the state income tax on federally taxable military retirement pay to members of the U.S. Army, Navy, Air Force, Marines, Coast Guard, and Army and Air National Guard.

Property Tax Exemptions
Veterans, who have ninety days of wartime service, including Merchant Marines, who served during WWII, are eligible for a $1,500 exemption for property tax purposes (e.g., real property or automobiles). You have the option to choose to apply this exemption to your real estate or automobile tax. Certain veterans, who do not own real property or a motor vehicle, may be eligible for a tax refund if they are leasing a motor vehicle.

Veterans below a certain income level and/or service connected disabled veterans are eligible for additional property tax exemptions (up to $10,000 for paraplegics). Surviving spouses of veterans may also be eligible for this benefit. Contact your municipality's Tax Assessor Officer for specific details.

By Connecticut's definition, this exemption is the reduction of the property's assessed value for tax purposes.

Connecticut Financial Assistance Benefits

The Soldiers', Sailors' and Marines' Fund
The Soldiers', Sailors' and Marines' Fund (SSMF) is a state fund administered by the American Legion for the purpose of providing temporary financial assistance for veterans with ninety days of wartime service, who are disabled, unemployed or for sickness. An applicant must be a resident of the State of Connecticut at the time of application for benefits. SSMF provides funding for emergency needs such as clothing, food, medical and surgical aid, and general care and relief. For further information please call 860-296-0719.

Connecticut State Employment Benefits

Employment Assistance
An employee who leaves any public authority or public agency to enter the armed forces can be reinstated in their former position. Veterans must reapply within ninety days following receipt of a certificate from the armed forces confirming satisfactory service.

For classified competitive state exams, a wartime veteran eligible for or receiving VA compensation receives an additional ten points. A wartime veteran not eligible for VA compensation or pension receives five additional points. A spouse of a qualified veteran is also eligible for additional points. However, to qualify, the veteran or spouse must achieve a passing grade on the examination score. If an honorably discharged veteran has served in a military action for which he/she received, or is entitled to receive, a campaign badge or expeditionary medal, he/she qualifies for five additional points if they receive a passing grade on their examination.

On a competitive municipal examination, a wartime veteran eligible for VA compensation or a pension, who has received a passing score, receives ten additional points.

A wartime veteran not eligible for compensation or a pension, who has received a passing score, receives five additional points.

Connecticut Veteran Education Benefits

Educational Benefit/Tuition Waivers
State law provides that tuition fees at state educational institutions be waived for certain veterans and certain dependents.

 Approved institutions for this benefit are:

- State Regional Community/Technical Colleges
- State Universities

In order to be eligible for a tuition waiver, one must:

- Be a veteran who served 90 days of active duty during a period of war as defined in; and
- Have been accepted to an approved institution; and
- Be a Connecticut resident at the time of acceptance to the institution.
- A veteran's dependents can also qualify for tuition waiver if the veteran is declared missing in action while serving in the armed forces after January 1, 1960.

High School Diplomas and Veterans of WWII
Local Boards of Education may award diplomas to those WWII veterans who did not receive them when they left high school before graduation for military service

Other Connecticut State Veteran Benefits

Burial in Connecticut's Veterans' Cemetery
Any veteran discharged with other than a dishonorable discharge is eligible for burial in a state veterans' cemetery. Spouses are also eligible for this benefit.

Motor Vehicles Waiver
State law provides for free motor vehicle registration and special plates to former prisoners of war and recipients of the Medal of Honor.

Veterans, who were state residents at the time of induction and who apply within two years of receiving an honorable discharge, are exempt from paying for an operator's license and examination fees for one licensing period.

State law also provides that fees may be waived for the following registration items, subject to a formal determination by the Department of Motor Vehicles:

- Special License plates for disabled veterans
- Special fee license plates for certain disabilities (loss of use or loss of limb, or blind) handicapped and overtime parking.
- If receiving auto grant from the VA or Medal of Honor recipient, exemption from registration fees.

Retirement
Members of The Municipal Employees' Retirement System, who leave municipal employment to enter the armed forces while the United States is at war, engaged in hostilities, or during national emergencies and are re-employed by the municipality within six months of discharge, are credited with the period of service as though they had been continuously employed. This six-month limitation can be extended due to service-related disability.

Delaware State Veteran's Benefits

The state of Delaware provides several veteran benefits. This section offers a brief description of each of the following benefits.

- Housing Benefits
- Financial Assistance Benefits
- Employment Benefits
- Education Benefits
- Other State Veteran Benefits

Delaware Veteran Housing Programs

State Veterans Home Fund
The Delaware Veterans Home Fund provides for individuals who claim an overpayment of taxes on their income tax return to voluntarily designate a tax deductible contribution to the Veterans Home. The fund will be used for the construction, operation and maintenance of a Veterans Home in the State of Delaware.

Delaware Financial Assistance Benefits

Pension Benefits for Paraplegic Veterans
Each paraplegic veteran eligible for benefits hereunder shall receive a pension from the State of $3,000 per year payable in equal monthly installments at the end of each month in which such veteran is eligible. The veteran must file evidence with the Pension Office that: he/she is a paraplegic and fully disabled to the extent that he/she has no voluntary control over either of

his/her legs, and he/she is listed on the rolls of the U.S. Veterans Administration as totally disabled for the cause, and the disability is a direct result of service in the armed forces of the United States while the United States was officially at war or during a period when the United States was engaged in hostilities with another nation as a member of the United Nations.

Persons under age 60 receiving pensions from employers, the United States, the State or any subdivision thereof, may deduct up to $2,000 off of their federal adjusted gross income. Amounts received as pension by persons age 60 or older from employers, the United States, the State or any subdivision thereof may deduct up to $12,500 off of their federal adjusted gross income.

Delaware Veteran Employment Benefits

State Employment Veterans Preference
The rules shall provide for preference to be given to veterans of the armed forces of the U.S. who served during wartime. Such rules shall provide that: Preference shall be confined to original entrance and shall not be applied to promotion within the classified service or to retention in case of reduction in force; Preference shall be granted only in the form of credits to be added to earned ratings in examinations, with disabled veterans receiving no more than 10 points and other veterans no more than 5 points. A definition of a disabled veteran shall be set forth in the rules; All veterans shall be required to obtain a passing examination mark before preference credits. Employees in the classified service who, while in good standing, leave or have left the state service to engage in military service shall be given credit for seniority purposes for the time served in the armed forces not to exceed three years. Any preference points for which a veteran would qualify after complying with the provisions above, may be claimed by his or her unmarried widow or widower providing he or she achieves a passing examination grade.

Tax Credit for Employers Hiring Veterans
Delaware Governor Jack Markell has signed a bill giving tax credits to those who hire veterans. The new Veteran's Tax Credit in Delaware will be 10 percent of a qualified veteran's wages, up to a maximum of $1,500. Employers may take the credit the year a veteran is hired and the two subsequent tax years. According to the new law, a "qualified veteran" is anyone who has served in a hostile environment such as Iraq and Afghanistan.

Delaware Veteran Education Benefits

Educational Benefits For Children Of Deceased Veterans, Etc.
The State of Delaware provides educational benefits for the children of deceased veterans of the military services of the United States, military service personnel held prisoner of war and military service personnel officially declared to be missing in action. In order to qualify for this entitlement an applicant shall be: the child of a member of the armed forces who was killed while on active duty or who died from disease, wounds, injuries or disabilities arising or resulting from performance of duty; a member of the armed forces who is being held, or who was held prisoner of war; or a member of the armed forces officially declared missing in action; a person who at the time of application for benefits is at least 16 years of age, but not more than 24 years of age, and who shall have been a resident of the State for at least three years prior to the date of application; attending or admitted for attendance at an educational

institution beyond the high school level in a program not to exceed four years in duration. The per pupil benefits may include funds for the payment of room, board, tuition and required institutional fees for an academic year. Benefits shall be limited to four years of training or education. The amount of benefit per pupil shall not exceed $525 per year or the amount of tuition per academic year, whichever is greater. Benefits are administered by the Delaware Postsecondary Education Commission.

Education Benefits For Active Members Of The Delaware National Guard
Any active member of a federally recognized unit of the Delaware National Guard, who meets the requirements for satisfactory membership as defined by the Adjutant General of the Delaware National Guard, shall be eligible for funding support by the Delaware National Guard for certain post-secondary education tuition and fees.

High School Diploma For WWII Veterans
House Bill No. 60 provides a High School Diploma to those World War II veterans who did not graduate from high school due to their military service. Any World War II veteran who performed wartime service between December 7, 1941 - December 31, 1946 shall be eligible to receive a High School Diploma.

Other Delaware State Veteran Benefits

Copies of Statement of Service
The Delaware Commission of Veterans Affairs has established a repository for veterans' "Statement of Service" or similar documentary verification of active armed service. Records maintained are World War I through the Vietnam era. In 1987 the State of Delaware again started keeping records and have records from 1987 to present.

Free Death Certificates for Veterans
The State Registrar shall furnish free of charge to the relative of a veteran, one time, a certified copy of the veteran's certificate of death providing that said certified copy is essential to the settlement of a claim involving the settlement of the veteran's affairs. All other copies shall be issued at the statutory fee.

No Charge for Notary Services for Veterans
Service organizations' appointed notaries public may notarize documents and papers in connection with and for the benefit of any veteran, their families, or dependents. These notaries public shall make no charge for any service rendered in connection with filing claims on behalf of the veteran, their families, or dependents. The Delaware Commission of Veterans Affairs provides free notary service.

Veterans Preference - Admission to Governor Bacon Health Center
The Department of Health and Social Services shall give veterans of World War I, World War II, the Korean Conflict and the Vietnam era who are eligible for admission to the Health Center a preference over other persons with respect to admission thereto.

Delaware Veterans Memorial Cemetery
Veterans and members of the Armed Forces of the U.S. who qualify under the following:

1. Honorable Military Service
2. Legal Residence In Delaware
3. The Spouse Widow, Widower Or Dependent Minor Children

Indigent Veteran Burial

The Adjutant General shall provide out of funds appropriated to the Delaware National Guard for the proper interment of each and every indigent soldier, sailor or marine who shall have served in the Army, Marines, Navy or Air Force of the U.S. in any war in which it has been engaged and been honorably discharged there from, who shall at the time of his or her death be a resident of this State leaving insufficient means to defray the expenses of interment.

Special License Plates

Special License Plates For Former Prisoners Of War, Missing-In-Action, Purple Heart Recipients, Disabled Veterans, Members Of The Delaware National Guard & Reserves, Valor, Retired Military & Korean War Veterans.

The owner of any private passenger vehicle or a truck with a 3/4 ton or less manufacturer's rated capacity may apply to the Department of Transportation for the assignment to that vehicle of a special Prisoner-of-War (POW), Missing-in-Action (MIA), Purple Heart or disabled veteran (DAV) registration number.

Registration and Inspection of Motor Vehicles of Disabled Veterans

Any motor vehicle owned by a disabled veteran who shall ever have been eligible for 'adaptive equipment' benefits under Title 38 U.S.C. (which includes, but is not limited to power steering, power brakes, power window lifts, power seats, and special equipment necessary to assist the eligible person into and out of the automobile or other conveyance) shall be registered, but shall be exempted from the payment of registration fees, provided that such exemption shall be limited to one automobile per eligible veteran at any one time. The Division of Motor Vehicles shall furnish, without cost, number and registration plates for all such vehicles of such design as will distinguish them from other plates for which fees are paid. Nothing herein contained shall be construed as exempting such vehicles from the requirement of inspection.

Credited Military Service; Eligibility

Credited service for veterans shall mean: Those who first became an employee before July 1, 1976, full-time active duty, not in excess of 5 years, in the armed forces of the U.S. during time of war or national emergency, provided that the individual became an employee within five years after completion of his or her tour of duty; or within five years after his or her completion of a course of professional or vocational training, if such course was begun within five years after completion of his or her tour of duty, except that the aforesaid five year period within which the individual must become an employee shall not apply to full-time officers and members of the National Guard of the State who were active members of the State Employee's Pension Plan on June 1, 1970.

Auctioneer and Book Agent Exemption for Veterans

No honorably discharged soldier or sailor shall be required to procure any license to follow the occupation of canvassing for the sale of books or for the occupation commonly known as that of "book agent" or for the occupation of auctioneer. The certificate of honorable discharge of any such soldier or sailor shall be conclusive evidence of the right of such soldier or sailor to follow the occupations herein before mentioned without having procured a license thereof.

Hunting, Trapping and Fishing Licenses
Any member of the armed forces of the United States of America while actually stationed within the State shall be deemed a resident of this State for the purpose of obtaining a license to hunt, trap and fish in this State. (Title 7, Chapter 5, Section 505) Any veteran having at least a 60% service-connected disability (certified by the Veterans Administration), or 65 years or older, or are blind, are exempt from the licensing requirements.

Florida State Veteran's Benefits

The state of Florida provides several veteran benefits. This section offers a brief description of each of the following benefits.

- Housing Benefits
- Employment Benefits
- Education Benefits
- Other State Veteran Benefits

Florida Veteran Housing Programs

Florida State Veterans' Homes Program
The Robert Jenkins, Jr. Assisted Living/Domiciliary Home is a 150-bed Assisted Living Facility (ALF) that provides a special combination of housing, personalized supportive services, and incidental medical care to eligible veterans. Domiciliary care is provided to veterans discharged under honorable conditions. Veterans admitted must be residents of Florida for one year prior to admission and be in need of ALF care. Current admissions information is available through the office of the Home Administrator, County Veteran Service Office, or any of the FDVA offices listed.

Veterans' Nursing Homes of Florida
The Emory L. Bennett Veterans' Nursing Home in Daytona Beach (Volusia County) is a modern and progressive 120-bed facility providing skilled nursing home care and the highest quality of life and medical care to its veteran residents. The Baldomero Lopez Veterans' Nursing Home in Land O' Lakes (Pasco County), provides skilled nursing home care. Sixty of its 120 beds are for residents with dementia/ Alzheimer's disease. A beautiful park setting within the facility grounds is available for residents to enjoy the outdoors. Local veterans and civic groups donate many hours of their time volunteering and interacting with the residents at the Home. The Sandy Nininger Veterans' Nursing Home, in Pembroke Pines (Broward County) opened its doors to its first residents in June 2001. This 120-bed facility accommodates 60 residents with dementia disease. Each dementia/Alzheimer's module has a dining area, a small nutrition area, a centrally located living area, and a screened porch with a gated garden. The Clifford Sims Veterans' Nursing Home, in Springfield (Bay County) accepted its first resident in October 2003. This 120-bed facility offers skilled nursing home and dementia care.

The Douglas Jacobson Veterans' Nursing Home, in Port Charlotte (Charlotte County), opened in January 2004. This 120-bed facility offers skilled nursing home and dementia care. Basic admission requirements for all veterans' nursing homes in Florida include an honorable discharge, Florida residency for one year prior to admission, and certification of need of nursing home care by a VA physician.

Homestead Exemption (Permanent &Totally Disabled)
Any real estate used and owned as a homestead by a veteran who was honorably discharged with a service-connected permanent and total disability and for whom a letter from the United States Government or VA or its predecessor has been issued certifying that the veteran is totally and permanently disabled is exempt from taxation, provided the veteran is a permanent resident of the state on January 1 of the tax year for which exemption is being claimed or on January 1 of the year the veteran died.

The production by a veteran or the spouse or surviving spouse of a letter of total and permanent disability from the United States Government or VA or its predecessor before the property appraiser of the county in which property of the veteran lies shall be prima facie evidence of the fact that the veteran or the surviving spouse is entitled to such exemption.

In the event the totally and permanently disabled veteran pre-deceases his or her spouse and upon the death of the veteran, the spouse holds the legal or beneficial title to the homestead and permanently resides thereon as specified in FS 196.031, the exemption from taxation shall carry over to the benefit of the veteran's spouse until such time as he or she remarries or sells or otherwise disposes of the property. If the spouse sells the property, an exemption not to exceed the amount granted from the most recent ad valorem tax roll may be transferred to his or her new residence as long as it is used as his or her primary residence and he or she does not remarry.

Veterans who are paraplegic, hemiplegic, are permanently and totally disabled, must use a wheelchair for mobility, or are legally blind are exempt from real estate taxation if gross annual household income does not exceed the adjusted maximum allowed. The veteran must be a resident of the State of Florida to qualify. Certificate of such disability from two licensed doctors of this state or from the VA or an award letter from the Social Security Administration to the property appraiser is prima facie evidence of entitlement to such exemption.

Homestead Exemption (10% to 100% BUT not Permanent in nature)
Eligible veterans with service-connected disabilities of 10% or more shall be entitled to a $5000 property tax exemption. To qualify for homestead exemption a veteran must be a bonafide resident of the state.

Every person who is entitled to homestead exemption in this state and who is serving in any branch of the Armed Forces of the United States may file a claim for homestead exemption. Servicemen unable to file in person may file through next of kin or duly authorized representatives.

Visit the Florida Department of Veterans Affairs website for contact information and benefits assistance.

Florida Employment Benefits

Veterans' Preference in Employment and Retention

The state and its political subdivisions shall give preference in employment and retention in government positions to veterans who served during a wartime period and separated under honorable conditions, or who are disabled veterans who have compensable service-connected disabilities as well as to a spouse or un-remarried veteran's widow or widower under certain circumstances.

For additional information concerning veterans' preference, visit the Florida VA's online Vet Preference Overview
or contact the Florida Department of Veterans' Affairs:
By phone at: (727) 319-7462, Facsimile (727) 319-7780 By email: postd@fdva.state.fl.us

Florida Military Family Employment Advocacy Program
The Military Family Employment Advocacy Program provides advocates located in Florida's One-Stop Career Centers for regions where military bases and communities are located. Persons eligible for assistance through this program include spouses and dependents of active-duty military personnel, activated Florida National Guard members, and activated military reservists. Approximately 37,000 military spouses, not including military spouses of mobilized National Guard Members/Reservists, currently live in Florida. An increase is projected in the military spouse population due to returning and reassigned military members and their families.

Florida Education Benefits

High School Diploma - Korean War Veterans
Effective July 1, 2002, Florida veterans who served during the Korean War may be eligible to receive a high school diploma. Senate Bill 292 provides for the award of a high school diploma to certain Korean War veterans who started high school between 1946 and 1950. Veterans who were inducted into the armed forces between June 1950 and January 1954 and scheduled to graduate between 1950 and 1954 are eligible recipients. The revised law amends s. 232.246, F. S., which originally awarded high school diplomas to World War II veterans.
Veterans who meet the following criteria will be eligible:

- must be a Florida resident;
- inducted into military service between June 1950 and January 1954;
- received an honorable discharge;
- started high school between 1946 and 1950; and
- scheduled to graduate from high school between 1950 and 1954.

Tuition Deferment
Available to any veteran or other eligible student covered under Title 38, U.S.C. Allows one tuition deferment each academic year and an additional deferment when a delay in benefits occurs.

Reduced Tuition for National Guard
Active Florida Guard members in good standing as of June 30, 1997 are exempt from payment of one-half of tuition and fees. Individuals who enlist in the Guard after June 30, 1997 are eligible for full exemption of tuition and fees. Contact your National Guard Unit for

details.

Education for Children Of Deceased Or Disabled Florida Veterans
The State of Florida provides scholarships for dependent children of Florida veterans or servicemen who died in action or died from service-connected diseases or disabilities, have been verified by the Florida Department of Veterans' Affairs as having service-connected 100% total and permanent disabilities, have been determined to have service-connected total and permanent disability ratings of 100% and are in receipt of disability retirement from any branch of the United States Armed Services, or are classified as prisoners of war or missing in action. Specific residency requirements apply and the veteran must have served during specific wars, conflicts or events.

Other Florida State Veteran Benefits

Certification of Discharge or Separation
The Clerk of the Circuit Court shall record, without cost to the veteran, certificates of discharge or separation form the Armed Forces of the United States.

Disabled Veteran Identification Card
The Department of Veterans' Affairs may issue an identification card to any veteran who is a permanent resident of the state and who has been adjudged by the United States Department of Veterans Affairs or its predecessor to have a 100-percent, service-connected permanent and total disability rating for compensation, this could also be a rating of Individual Unemployability from the VA, or who has been determined to have a service-connected total and permanent disability rating of 100 percent and is in receipt of disability retirement pay from any branch of the United States Armed Services, upon the written request of such veteran. Such card may be used by the veteran as proof of eligibility for any benefit provided by state law for 100-percent, service-connected permanently and totally disabled veterans except this card may not be used as proof of eligibility for Exemption of Homesteads. The identification card shall bear a statement that it is unlawful for any person other than the veteran to whom it was issued to use the card.

Hunting and Fishing License
In order to receive a no-cost Resident Disabled Person's Hunting and Fishing Certificate from the Florida Fish and Wildlife Conservation Commission, applicants must attach a copy of one of the following certifying him or her as totally and permanently disabled:

- Certification by the U.S. Railroad Retirement Board
- Certification by the U.S. Department of Veterans Affairs or any branch of the U.S. Armed Forces
- A Florida Department of Veterans' Affairs 100% Service-connected Disabled Veteran Identification Card (must have a statement of "total and permanent disabled")
- Florida Department of Labor and Employment Security/AWI Division of Workers Compensation (LES Form DWC-4)
- An order from a Judge of Compensation claims
- Written confirmation by the carrier providing Workers' Compensation benefits OR

- Documentation of current (dated within the last 12 months) eligibility for Disability Benefits from Social Security Administration.

Applicants must also attach proof of Florida residency as outlined on the application.

No license shall be required for military service personnel who are Florida residents while they are home on leave for periods of 30 days or less.

Active-duty and retired military Florida residents can get a low cost Military Gold Sportsman's License. The license covers hunting, freshwater and saltwater fishing and a variety of associated permits at a greatly reduced cost. The Military Gold Sportsman's License is available at tax collectors' offices only. Applicants must present a current military ID card plus a Florida driver's license or orders showing they are stationed in Florida as proof of eligibility.

Motor Vehicle Military License Plates
Joining the 'Florida Salutes Veterans' and the U.S. Marine Corps license plates already available are new plates for the Army, Navy, Air Force, and the Coast Guard.

Check with your county tax collector to purchase your specialty plate. These tags are among the most affordable and patriotic specialty tags available. $15 of the $17 purchase price goes to the Veterans' Homes Trust Fund for maintenance and operation of Florida's five state veterans' nursing homes and one state veterans' domiciliary home.

Disabled Veteran Motor Vehicle License Plate
One free motor vehicle license number plate shall be issued by the department for use on any motor vehicle owned or leased by any disabled veteran who has been a continuous resident of Florida for the last five years or has established a domicile upon application accompanied by proof that:

1. the vehicle was acquired through financial assistance from the VA, or

2. the veteran has been determined by the VA to have a service-connected disability of 100% rating for compensation, or

3. the veteran has been determined to have a service- connected disability of 100% and is in receipt of disability retirement pay from any branch of the uniformed Armed Forces. A plate fee is charged.

Permits/Fees (parking, tolls, building improvements)
No totally and permanently disabled veteran who is a resident of Florida shall be required to pay license or permit fees to any county or municipality in order to make certain improvements to assist with his or her disability on any mobile home owned by the veteran and used as his/her residence. Improvements are limited to ramps, widening of doors, and similar improvements for the purpose of making the mobile home habitable for veterans confined to wheelchairs.

Handicapped Toll Permit - Any handicapped person who has a valid driver's license, who operates a vehicle specially equipped for use by the handicapped, and who is certified by a licensed physician or by the VA Adjudication Officer as being physically disabled and having permanent impairments which impair the person's ability to deposit coins in toll baskets shall be allowed to pass free through all tollgates. A vehicle window sticker will be issued.

Exemption Parking Permit: Persons With Permanent Mobility Problems - A disabled veteran who is a resident of this state and honorably discharged, and has been determined by the VA or the Federal Government to have a service-connected disability rating for compensation of 50% or greater and has a signed physician's statement of qualification is eligible for the permit. The fees are $1.50 for the initial parking permit, and $1.50 for renewal parking permit and for each additional renewal parking permit. The fee must be paid to the tax collector of the county in which the fee was generated. The department shall not issue to any one eligible applicant more than two exemption parking permits upon request of the applicant.

Homeless Veterans Program
About one-third of the adult homeless population have served their country in the Armed Services. On any given day, as many as 250,000 veterans (male and female) are living on the streets or in shelters, and perhaps twice as many experience homelessness at some point during the course of a year. Many other veterans are considered near homeless or at risk because of their poverty, lack of support from family and friends, and dismal living conditions in cheap hotels or in overcrowded or substandard housing.

Right now, the number of homeless male and female Vietnam era veterans is greater than the number of service persons who died during that war -- and a small number of Desert Storm veterans are also appearing in the homeless population. At this time, scientific studies indicate that there is no known, direct connection between military service, service in Vietnam, or exposure to combat and any increased risk of becoming homeless. Family background, access to support from family and friends, and various personal characteristics (rather than military service) seem to be the stronger indicators of risk of homelessness.

Almost all homeless veterans are male (about three percent are women), the vast majority are single, and most come from poor, disadvantaged backgrounds. Homeless veterans tend to be older and more educated than homeless non-veterans. But similar to the general population of homeless adult males, about 45% of homeless veterans suffer from mental illness and (with considerable overlap) slightly more than 70% suffer from alcohol or other drug abuse problems. Roughly 56% are African American or Hispanic.

Benefits Counseling
The FDVA has state Veterans' Claims Counselors co-located with the VA in the Bay Pines Regional Office, and in each VA Medical Center and VA Outpatient Clinic in Florida. Assistance with claims is free (membership is not required) and covers all state and federal veterans' programs.

Commission as a Notary Public
The usual fee shall not be required for the issuance of a Commission as a Notary Public to a veteran who served during a period of wartime service, and who has been rated 50% or more for service-connected disability. Other fees may apply.

Georgia State Veteran's Benefits

The state of Georgia provides several veteran benefits. This section offers a brief description of each of the following benefits.

- Housing Benefits
- Tax Benefits

- Employment Benefits
- Education Benefits
- Other State Veteran Benefits

Georgia Veteran Housing Programs

War Veterans Homes
Treatment is provided at no charge to all honorably discharged war Veterans in the Georgia War Veterans Home, Milledgeville, and in the Georgia War Veterans Nursing Home in Augusta. The term "war Veteran" for this benefit means any Veteran who served on active duty in the armed forces of the United States, or on active duty in a reserve component, including the National Guard, during wartime or during the period January 31, 1955, through May 7, 1975. To determine eligibility for admission, see your local SDVS office.

Georgia Veterans Tax Benefits

Exemption from Homestead Tax
Homestead Tax: Certain disabled veterans and certain widows/widowers, or minor children are allowed the maximum amount which may be granted under United States Code.

Exemption from Sales Tax on Vehicles
A disabled Veteran who receives a VA grant for the purchase and special adapting of a vehicle is exempt from paying the state sales tax on the vehicle (only on the original grant).

Ad Valorem Tax on Vehicles
Exemption for Veterans who are verified by VA to be 100 percent totally and permanently service-connected disabled and Veterans who are receiving or who are entitled to receive statutory awards from VA for: (1) loss or permanent loss of use of one or both feet; (2) loss or permanent loss of use of one or both hands; (3) loss of sight in one or both eyes; or (4) permanent impairment of vision of both eyes to a prescribed degree. Exemption is granted on the vehicle the Veteran owns or leases and upon which the free Disabled Veterans (DV) Motor Vehicle license plate is attached.

Exemption from State Income Tax
The period of time military personnel served on active duty as members of the armed forces of the United States in combat activities during a period designated by the President plus the next 180 days thereafter are disregarded in determining whether any filing requirement has been performed within the time limit prescribed for filing.

For individuals who are hospitalized as a result of an injury or confined as a prisoner-of-war, the period of service in the combat zone, plus the period of confinement and the next 180 days there after shall be disregarded in determining whether any filing requirement has been performed within the time limit prescribed for filing.

Certificate of Exemption
Disabled Veterans are exempt from payment of occupational taxes, administration fees, and regulatory fees imposed by local governments for peddling, conducting a business, or

practicing a profession or semi profession.

Eligibility: Veterans must (1) be discharged under honorable conditions from the armed forces of the United States; (2) have 10 percent physical disability for certain wartime Veterans or a 25 percent service-connected physical disability for peace time-only Veterans; and (3) have an income that is not liable for state income taxes.

Abatement of State Income Taxes
Georgia law provides that service personnel who die as a result of wounds, disease or injury incurred while serving in a combat zone as a member of the armed forces of the United States, are exempt from all Georgia income taxes for the taxable year of his or her death, nor shall such taxes apply for any prior taxable year ending on or after the first day he/she served in the combat zone.

Georgia Employment Benefits

Employment Preference
Extended to Veterans employed under the State Merit System.

(a) Any veteran who has served on active duty as a member of the armed forces of the United States for a period of more than 180 days, not counting service under an initial period of active duty for training under the six-months' reserve or National Guard programs, any portion of which service occurred during a period of armed conflict in which any branch of the armed forces of the United States engaged, whether under United States command or otherwise, and who was honorably discharged there from shall be entitled to and shall have five points added to his passing score on any competitive civil service examination for employment with the state government or any political subdivision thereof; provided, however, that such veteran is not already eligible for veterans preference under Article IV, Section III, Paragraph II of the Constitution of Georgia.

(b) Notwithstanding the 180 day minimum active duty requirement of subsection (a) of this Code section, the five-point preference granted to veterans under said subsection shall apply to any member of the National Guard or armed forces reserve who served on active duty for any length of time during any portion of the time the armed forces of the United States were engaged in Operation Desert Shield or Operation Desert Storm if such service occurred in an area of imminent danger as defined by the United States Department of Defense.

(c)Any veteran, as above, who has at least a 10 percent service connected disability, as rated and certified by the United States Department of Veterans Affairs, shall be entitled to and shall have ten points added to his passing score on any competitive civil service examination, said ten-point preference being in lieu of and not in addition to any other similar preference accorded by law.

Employment Assistance
State employees receive 18 days of military leave per year.
Eligibility: Georgia National Guard member.

Georgia Education Benefits

Georgia Military Scholarship
The State of Georgia offers 39 "Full Ride" scholarships per year to attend North Georgia.

The scholarship pays for room, meals, tuition, uniforms, and fees. It also provides a $375 a semester stipend for books.

In addition, GMS recipients receive National Guard weekend drill pay, GI Bill, GI Bill "kicker", pay for attending Army basic and advanced training, an enlistment bonus of up to $20,000, and Army ROTC contract pay (upon contracting at the beginning of the sophomore year).

After graduating college you will receive a $10,000 commissioning bonus.

In order to be considered for the scholarship, you must be nominated by your local Georgia state assemblyman. Deadline for the application is March 15.

Scholarship Requirements:

1. Be a resident of Georgia.
2. Receive a nomination by a State Legislator.
3. Have a minimum critical reading score of 480 and math of 440 on the SAT, have a 3.0 cumulative GPA on a 4.0 scale, and graduate high school with a college prep or dual seal diploma.
4. Meet Army National Guard mental and physical standards.
5. Agree to serve as an enlisted member in the Georgia Army National Guard while a student at North Georgia.
6. Agree to accept a commission upon graduation from North Georgia and serve four years as a commissioned officer in the Georgia Army National Guard.

Learn more about Georgia State Veterans Benefits

Tuition Assistance (Georgia Air National Guard)
Up to 100% tuition is paid, not to exceed $2,790 per school year, $1,395 per semester or the rate of $116.25 per semester hour. Rate per quarter hour not to exceed $77.40.

Eligibility: Georgia Air National Guard member.

The National Guard Service Cancelable Loan Fund
Provides up to 100% of the tuition charges; not to exceed the current academic year "per semester maximum." Soldiers with a baccalaureate degree are not eligible for this program.

Eligibility: Must be a legal resident of Georgia and be a member in good standing of the Georgia National Guard. Loan is repaid through continued membership and good standing in the Guard.

Georgia HERO Scholarship
The Georgia HERO (Helping Educate Reservists and their Offspring) Scholarship Program was created to provide educational grant assistance to members of the Georgia National

Guard and U.S. Military Reservists who served in combat zones or the children of such members of the Georgia National Guard and U.S. Military Reserves. The grant is to attend an approved school for a maximum of up to four award years in the sum of $2,000.00 per award year. No person shall be eligible to receive grant assistance provided under this subsection in excess of $8,000.00.

Other Georgia State Veteran Benefits

Hunting and Fishing Licenses
Any veteran who is a legal resident of Georgia, who files with the Game and Fish Division, Department of Natural Resources a letter from VA or a certificate from the Social Security Administration, Medicaid, Medicare, Railroad Retirement System or a unit of federal, state or local government recognized by the Board of Natural Resources by rule or regulation stating that he/she is a totally and permanently disabled veteran, is entitled to a lifetime honorary hunting and fishing license allowing the veteran to fish and hunt within the state without the payment of any fee. Persons who are at least 65 years old or who are rated totally blind also qualify.

Honorary Veteran's Hunting/Fishing License
The One-Time Honorary Veterans License is valid for 12 months from the date of issue. The Honorary Veterans License covers all recreational hunting and fishing licenses (except Federal Duck Stamp).

This specifically includes: Alligator, Hunting, Primitive Weapons, Big Game, WMA, Georgia Waterfowl Conservation, Fishing and Trout licenses. It does not include commercial licenses.

Applicants for the Honorary Veterans License must be military veterans who meet all of the following criteria:
- Have not previously received this license.
- Served on active Federal duty for 90 or more days.
- Discharge date is July 1, 2005 or later (veterans discharged before July 1, 2005 are not eligible for this license).
- Currently reside in Georgia.

Visit the Georgia Wildlife website for application and further details.

In addition Veterans have the benefit of purchasing a Georgia State Sportsman's Lifetime License at a reduced cost of $400. Learn more.

Veterans Drivers' Licenses
Issued at no charge to eligible Veterans and National Guard or Reservists with 20 or more years of service.

Eligibility: Driver's license issued without charge to: (1) Veterans who were residents of Georgia at the time of enlistment or commissioning and are residents at the time of application for the license or who have been residents of Georgia for at least two years immediately preceding the date of application for the license. Individuals must have served on active duty in the armed forces of the United States or on active duty in a reserve component, including the National Guard, during wartime or any conflict when personnel were committed by the President, except for periodic transfer from reserve status to active duty status for training purposes, and who were discharged or separated under honorable conditions. The individual need not have been assigned to a unit or division which directly participated in such war or conflict. (2) any member or former member of the National Guard or reserve forces who has 20 or more years creditable service.

Honorary Driver's License
Issued without charge to: (1) any Georgia resident who is the surviving spouse of a Veteran who was eligible for a Veteran?s license, so long as the surviving spouse does not remarry; or (2) any resident of Georgia who is the spouse of a Veteran who would qualify for a Veteran?s license were it not for the Veteran?s permanent disabilities which preclude the operation of a motor vehicle.

Vehicle License Tags
Medal of Honor Tags: Special license plates are issued without charge to a Veteran who is a legal resident of Georgia and who is a Medal of Honor recipient. Two distinctive license plates will be issued to be placed on the front and rear of the motor vehicle owned by the Medal of Honor recipient.

Free Disabled Veteran Tags (Automobile/Motorcycle): Provided at no charge to: (1) any Veteran who was separated under honorable conditions and who served on active duty in the armed forces or on active duty in a reserve component, including the National Guard, and who is receiving or entitled to receive a statutory award from VA for (a) loss or permanent loss of use of one or both feet; (b) loss or permanent loss of use of one or both hands; (c) loss of sight in one or both eyes; or (d) permanent impairment of both eyes to the extent that there is central visual acuity of 20/200 if there is a field defect in which the peripheral field has contracted to such an extent that the widest diameter of visual field subtends an angular distance no greater than 20 degrees in the better eye; or (2) any Veteran separated under honorable conditions and verified by VA as receiving or entitled to receive compensation at the 100 percent rate as a result of being totally disabled permanently or totally disabled non-permanently.

Georgia law allows a disabled Veteran to obtain only one license plate at no charge. It can be placed on either a leased or owned vehicle.

Paid Disabled Veteran Tags: Disabled Veteran tags are available to Veterans who were separated under honorable conditions and who meet the same degree of disability which is required for the issuance of Free DV tags, but are unable to qualify for a free license plate. These DV tags are not issued free but may be purchased at regular license plate rates.

POW Tags: One license plate will be issued at no charge to any Veteran who is a former prisoner-of-war, who was discharged under honorable conditions, and who is a legal resident of Georgia. Former prisoners-of-war are exempt from paying ad valorem taxes for state, county, municipal and school purposes on the vehicle on which they place the no charge POW license plate. Additional plates may be purchased upon payment of the appropriate taxes and registration fees. A widow/widower of a deceased former POW is eligible for the issuance of a free POW tag so long as they remain unmarried.

Purple Heart Tags: Recipients of the Purple Heart medal are entitled to one license plate at no charge. Additional tag(s) can be obtained by paying the regular license fees plus a manufacturing fee.

Pearl Harbor Tags: Veterans of the armed forces of the United States who survived the attack on Pearl Harbor are eligible to receive a special and distinctive vehicle license plate upon application and payment of an additional fee.

Veterans License Tags: Retired personnel of the U.S. Armed Forces or individuals who served during WWI, WWII, Korean War, Vietnam War, Operation Desert Shield/Storm, Operation Enduring Freedom, and Operation Iraqi Freedom are eligible to purchase special and distinctive vehicle license plates. All requests must be accompanied by payment of the appropriate taxes, registration fees and manufacturing fees. Motor Vehicle owners who retired from active duty with the Armed Forces of the United States shall be issued one retired tag at no charge upon applications.

ID Cards
Personal identification cards are available to Veterans who do not have a motor vehicle driver's license and who would, otherwise, be entitled to issuance of a Veteran?s driver's license.

Reduced Fees for Disabled Veterans
Any service connected disabled Veteran who was discharged under honorable conditions can visit/use state parks historical sites and recreational areas at reduced rates. A 25% reduced fee for all facilities, lodging, and any recreational activities in the State of Georgia will be granted by the park upon presentation of the entitlement card.

Eligibility: Veteran who is a legal resident of the State of Georgia and has been certified by DVA as a disabled veteran. For this purpose, a disabled veteran is a veteran who has been discharged under honorable conditions from any branch of the armed forces of the United States and has a physical disability that was incurred during the period of service in the armed forces.

Veterans License Plates
Retired personnel of the U.S. Armed Forces or individuals who served during WWI, WWII, Korean War, Vietnam War, Operation Desert Shield/Storm, Operation Enduring Freedom, and Operation Iraqi Freedom are eligible to purchase special and distinctive vehicle license plates. All requests must be accompanied by payment of the appropriate taxes, registration fees and manufacturing fees. Motor Vehicle owners who retired from active duty with the Armed Forces of the United States shall be issued one free tag upon applications.

Handicapped Parking
Holders of DV license tags are authorized to park their vehicles displaying such tags in parking areas designated for the handicapped without obtaining special handicapped parking area permits. This does not apply to federal parking areas.

Motor Fuel Service to Handicap
When there is an option on the price of fuel at a full-service/self-service facility, a station

employee, upon request will dispense fuel at the lower price from the self-service pump into vehicles bearing HV or DV license tags if: (1) the handicapped/disabled Veteran is driving the vehicle into which fuel is to be dispensed; and (2) the Veteran is not accompanied by a person at least 16 years of age who is not blind or has impaired mobility.

Guardianship
The Uniform Guardianship Act provides for appointment of a guardian for incompetent Veterans and for Veterans? children when VA benefits are involved. These appointments are made on the basis of certificates issued only by VA.

Vital Statistics
Veterans, dependents, VA or Veterans? organizations, may obtain copies of marriage, divorce, birth and death documents without charge, through the Department of Veterans Service, provided the copies are to be used for establishing disability or death claims with VA, and the request is in writing.

Service Records
There is no charge for recording of Veterans? discharge certificates (DD Form 214) in county Superior Courts.

Assistance
All Georgia Veterans and their dependents are urged to visit the nearest office of the Georgia Department of Veterans Service for complete information on benefits for which they may be eligible as well as professional assistance in obtaining them.

Cemeteries
Any member of the Armed Forces who is a veteran under the rules established by the U.S. Department of Veterans Affairs, and was separated under other than dishonorable conditions, and who has been a resident of Georgia for at least two years immediately preceding his/her death is eligible for burial in the Georgia Veterans Memorial Cemetery in Milledgeville or in the Georgia Veterans Memorial Cemetery that will open soon in Glennville.

Hawaii State Veteran's Benefits

The state of Hawaii provides several veteran benefits. This section offers a brief description of each of the following benefits.

- Housing Benefits
- Financial Assistance Benefits
- Employment Benefits
- Other State Veteran Benefits

Hawaii Veteran Housing Programs

Special Housing for Disabled Veterans
Payment by the State of up to $5,000 to each qualified, totally disabled veteran for the purpose of purchasing or remodeling a home to improve handicapped accessibility.

Hawaii Financial Assistance Benefits

Tax Exemptions

Applies to real property that is owned and occupied as a home by a totally disabled veteran or their widow(er). Also applies to passenger cars when they are owned by totally disabled veterans and subsidized by the Department of Veterans Affairs.

Hawaii Employment Benefits

Employment and Re-employment
Preference is given to veterans, Vietnam-era veterans, service-connected, disabled veterans and their widow(er)s for civil service positions, training programs, job counseling and referrals to civilian jobs by the Workforce Development Division, Department of Labor & Industrial Relations. Re-employment rights for veterans, Reservists or National Guard members who leave a position within State or County government for training or active military service.

Visit the Hawaii Office of Veterans Services website for contact information and benefits assistance.

Other Hawaii State Veteran Benefits

Burials
Burials for qualified veterans (including U.S. war allies) and their dependents in Veterans Cemeteries on Oahu, Hawaii, Kauai, Maui, Molokai, or Lanai.

Vital Statistics
Free certified copies of vital statistics forms when needed for veterans' claims.

License Plates
For the same cost as regular license plates, qualified veterans can acquire distinctive veterans' license plates for their car or motorcycle. Currently available are: "Veteran," "Combat," "Combat Wounded," "Pearl Harbor Survivor," "Former POW," "World War II Veteran" "Korean War Veteran," and "Vietnam Veteran."

Idaho State Veteran's Benefits

The state of Idaho provides several veteran benefits. This section offers a brief description of the housing and other State Veteran benefits offered in Idaho.

Idaho Veteran Housing Programs

Veterans Homes
The following are Veteran Homes located in Idaho:

- Boise Veterans Home

- Lewiston Veterans Home

- Pocatello Veterans Home

Applicants may be peacetime or wartime veterans, with wartime veterans retaining priority admission status. Applicants must have been discharged under honorable conditions and be a bona fide resident of the state of Idaho. In addition, applicants must be unemployable as a result of age, illness, or disability. Effective July 1, 2000, applicants must apply for and become eligible for Medicaid benefits or must pay the established maximum monthly nursing care charge.

Other Idaho State Veteran Benefits

Idaho State Parks Veterans Pass
Idaho Department of Parks and Recreation (IDPR) offers Veteran?s Pass that waives all camping fees for Idaho veterans who are 100% service-related disabled. This pass, which is wallet size, is good for one camping site per eligible veteran for his/her family. All an eligible Idaho veteran will typically need to pay a reservation fee and any utility hookups.

Idaho State Veterans Cemetery
The State of Idaho's Cemetery is located on 76.5 acres adjacent to the Dry Creek Cemetery. The site is just North of Hill Road and East of Horseshoe bend Road. The Terteling Company Donated approximately 40 acres in two parcels to the state and the remaining acreage was purchased from Dry Creek Cemetery District. The Cemetery was made possible by a grant from the Veterans Administration State Cemetery Grants Program and has funded 100% of the design, construction and equipment costs.

License Plates
$15 dollars from each new veteran's license plate and $5 dollars from each renewal goes to the operation and maintenance for the veterans Cemetery. Click on the license plate to purchase or get further information about the veteran's license plate.

Illinois State Veteran's Benefits

The state of Illinois provides several veteran benefits. This section offers a brief description of each of the following benefits.

- Housing Benefits
- Financial Assistance Benefits
- Employment Benefits
- Education Benefits
- Other State Veteran Benefits

Illinois Veteran Housing Programs

GI Loan for Heroes
The G-I Loan for Heroes is the new Illinois Homeownership Program for Veterans and Active Service Personnel. The G-I Loan offers significantly below market homeownership financing and counseling. There are two program packages, one for Veterans and one for active duty personnel.

Veterans' Program: The Veterans' Program is designed for honorably discharged Veterans who qualify under the income and purchase price limits of the IHDA MRB Program. Participants will receive a substantially below market rate financing package, closing cost assistance and homeownership counseling. In addition, under federal legislation passed in December 2006, Veterans do not have to be first-time homebuyers to qualify.

Active Duty Program: The Active Duty program is designed for active duty service personnel in the Armed Services and Reserve Forces. Under this program, they will receive the same package as the Veterans, except they must qualify as a first time homebuyer under the IHDA MRB Program.

Specially Adapted Housing
Assistance is provided for service-connected disabled veterans for the purpose of acquiring or remodeling suitable dwelling units with special fixtures or moveable facilities made necessary by the veteran's permanent and total service-connected disabilities.

Visit the Illinois Department of Veterans Affairs website for contact information and benefits assistance.

Illinois Financial Assistance Benefits

World War II Bonus Payment
A bonus of $10 per month for domestic service and $15 per month for foreign service is payable to a veteran who was a resident of Illinois at time of entering service, served at least 60 days on active duty between September 16, 1940 and September 3, 1945, and received an honorable discharge. Survivors are entitled to a benefit of $1,000, if the veteran's death was service-connected and within the period specified.

Korean, Vietnam and Persian Gulf Conflict Bonus
A $100 bonus is payable for service during one of the following periods:

Korea - June 27, 1950 - July 27, 1953
Vietnam - January 1, 1961 - March 28, 1973
Vietnam Frequent Wind - April 29, 30, 1975
Persian Gulf - August 2, 1990 - November 30, 1995

The claimant must also be in receipt of one of the following medals: Korean Service Medal, Vietnam Service Medal, Armed Forces Expeditionary Medal Vietnam Era or the Southwest Asia Service Medal; and have been a resident of Illinois for 12 months immediately prior to entering service and have received an Honorable Discharge. (Individuals currently on active duty who served in the Persian Gulf may apply prior to discharge by also including the "Armed Forces Certificate".)

Vietnam Veteran Survivors Compensation
Survivors are entitled to a payment of $1,000 if veteran's death is service-connected or is the direct result of service-connected disabilities incurred in the period specified. A separate application is required.

POW Compensation
Persons on active duty with the Armed Forces of the United States or employed by the United States Government on, or after, January 1, 1961, who were residents of Illinois 12 months prior to entry, and who were taken and held prisoner by hostile forces in Southwest Asia, are entitled to $50 for each month or portion thereof while being held captive.

Global War on Terrorism Survivors' Compensation
A $3,000 bonus is payable to survivors of certain persons killed by terrorist acts or hostile activities during performance of military service in periods recognized as wartime by United States campaign or service medals. Residency of 1 year in Illinois prior to entering military service is required.

Tax Exemption
This exemption is allowed on the assessed value of real property for which federal funds have been used for the purchase or construction of specially adapted housing for as long as the veteran, or the spouse, or unmarried surviving spouse resides on the property. The 2007 homestead legislation created two new exemptions for Veterans that take effect for the 2007 tax year:

The Returning Veterans' Homestead Exemption provides qualifying Veterans a one-time $5,000 reduction to their home's equalized assessed value (EAV). Qualifying Veterans who return from active duty in an armed conflict involving the U.S. armed forces can file an application upon their return home to receive this exemption.

The new Disabled Veterans' Standard Homestead Exemption provides a reduction in a property's EAV to a qualifying property owned by a Veteran with a service-connected disability certified by the U. S. Department of Veterans' Affairs. A $2,500 homestead exemption is available to a Veteran with a service-connected disability of at least 50% but less than 75% or a $5,000 homestead exemption is available to a veteran with a service connected disability of at least 75%. A disabled Veteran must file an annual application by the county's due date to continue to receive this exemption.

Tax Exemption for Mobile Home
This exemption applies to the tax imposed by the Mobile Home Local Services Tax Act when that property is owned and used exclusively by a disabled veteran, spouse or unmarried surviving spouse as a home. The veteran must have received authorization of the Specially Adapted Housing Grant by the USDVA, whether benefit was used or not. Applicant must be a permanent resident of the State of Illinois on January 1 of the tax year for which the exemption is being claimed. Disabled veterans that now live in a mobile home and never received the Specially Adapted Housing Grant are not eligible. Please contact your local service office for more information.

Illinois Employment Benefits

State Government/Employment Preference
Preference is given in Central Management Services entrance examinations to honorably discharged veterans who served in times of hostilities and peacetime. The Department of Central Management Services also conducts a Veterans Outreach Program that provides professional counseling to Veterans seeking state employment with the 45 boards, agencies, and commissions under the Governor's jurisdiction. Interested Veterans may learn more about the program or to begin the process of state employment by calling 1-800-643-8138.

Jobs for Vets
The Department of Employment Security/Illinois Job Service provides a trained "Veterans Representative" to help you get the training and job you need. An electronic statewide job search information system is available at different locations throughout the State of Illinois. Veterans should call 1-888-FOR-IETC to find their nearest Representative.

The Department of Human Services provides services for veterans with mental/physical disabilities that assist them in returning to gainful employment.

The Illinois Department of Commerce and Community Affairs have a number of Small Business Administration loan and Job Training Programs.

Illinois Education Benefits

Educational Opportunities for Children (10-18 Yrs)
Financial aid is provided annually to each child between the ages of 10 and 18 years of a veteran who died or became totally disabled as a result of service in the Armed Forces during World War I, or II, the Korean and Vietnam Conflicts or beginning February 1, 1955, until such individuals are no longer eligible for induction under the Universal Military Training and Service Act. The financial aid applies to a state educational institution of elementary grade, high school or vocational training school.

MIA/POW Scholarship
Dependents of a veteran who has been declared by the Department of Defense or U.S. Department of Veterans Affairs to be a prisoner of war; missing-in-action; to have died as the result of a service-connected disability; or be permanently disabled from service-connected

causes with 100% disability; and, who was an Illinois resident or was an Illinois resident within six months of entering service may be eligible for the scholarship. Eligible dependents are entitled to full payment of tuition and certain fees to any state supported Illinois institution of higher learning consisting of the equivalent of four (4) calendar years of full-time enrollment including summer terms (i.e., 120 points).

State Approving Agency
Approves training for veterans in the areas of higher education, apprenticeship training, vocational training, and on the job training.

Veterans' Grant
The Illinois Veteran Grant (IVG) Program pays tuition and certain fees at all Illinois state-supported colleges, universities and community colleges for Illinois residents. An individual must:

- be an honorably discharged veteran; and
- reside in Illinois six months before entering the service; and
- have at least one full year of active duty in the U.S. Armed Forces which includes veterans who were assigned to active duty in a foreign country in a time of hostilities in that country, regardless of length of service; and
- return to Illinois within six months of discharge from the service.

Illinois National Guard Scholarship
Any enlisted person or Lieutenant or Captain with at least one year service in the Illinois Army/Air National Guard may participate. Available for eight semesters or twelve quarters of full-time or part-time undergraduate study or graduate study at any Illinois state-controlled university or community college. Recipient is entitled to payment of tuition and certain fees.

Children of Veterans Scholarship
Each county in the state shall be entitled, annually, to one honorary scholarship at the University of Illinois, for the benefit of children of veterans of WWI, WWII, Korean War, the Vietnam Conflict and any time on or after August 2, 1990 and until those persons in service are no longer eligible for the Southwest Asia Service Medal. Preference is given to the children of deceased and disabled veterans. Such children shall be entitled to receive, without charge for tuition, instruction in any or all departments of the University for a term of at least four (4) consecutive years. Details may be obtained from the University's Financial Aid Office.

Other Illinois State Veteran Benefits

Cartage Fees

When the federal government has furnished a headstone or marker, the ILLINOIS DEPARTMENT OF VETERANS' AFFAIRS shall pay up to the allowable reimbursement amount for the setting of such marker within Illinois. Currently, the maximum amount is $100.00 payable upon approval of the application.

Graves Registration

The Illinois Department of Veterans' Affairs shall maintain a card file Roll of Honor of all veterans buried in the State of Illinois. Every person, firm or corporation owning or controlling any cemetery or burial place in this State is required to keep a permanent record of the burial of each U.S. war veteran or memorial marker erected for this purpose.

Indigent Veterans

The county Veterans Assistance Commission shall provide burial for any honorably discharged indigent veteran, or their mothers, fathers, spouse or surviving spouse, or minor children without sufficient means to defray the funeral expenses. The expense of such burial shall not exceed the sum of $600. Emergency food, transportation, etc. are provided in certain cases. Please contact your local county Veterans Assistance Commission for more information.

Camping & Admission Fees

This benefit provides for the exemption of camping and admission fees for certain disabled persons and former prisoners of war who are Illinois residents and wish to camp in parks under the control of the Illinois Department of Natural Resources. Documentation is required.

Hunting and Fishing Privileges

Fishing and hunting licenses are not required for disabled veterans receiving 10% or greater service-connected compensation, or total disability pension benefits. To acquire a permit, contact your local Veterans Service office.

State Fair

Honorably discharged veterans of all ages and their families shall be admitted FREE, when they properly identify themselves, on Veterans' Day at the fair. Veterans Day includes a day-long program of drum corps, drill teams, and color guard competition. Admission is FREE to people 60 and older on Senior Day.

Necessary Documents to File Claims

Certificate of Discharge DD 214, death certificate, marriage license, insurance policies and in some cases medical documentation.

Indiana State Veteran's Benefits

The state of Indiana provides several veteran benefits. This section offers a brief description of each of the following benefits.

- Housing Benefits

- Financial Assistance Benefits

- Employment Benefits

- Education Benefits

- Other State Veteran Benefits

Indiana Veteran Housing Programs

The Veterans Home
The Indiana Veterans Home in West Lafayette provides nursing and domiciliary care for any Hoosier Veteran with at least one day of wartime service. To qualify you must have been a resident of Indiana for at least three years. The Home is open to both veterans and their spouses.

The Indiana Soldiers and Sailors Children's Home
The Soldiers' and Sailors' Children's Home, located in Knightstown, provides for the care and education of the children of veterans and members of the active Armed Forces. There are entrance provisions for other relatives of veterans if space is available at the Home.

Visit the Indiana Department of Veterans Affairs website for contact information and benefits assistance.

Indiana Financial Assistance Benefits

Property Tax Abatements
Property tax deductions are available to disabled Hoosier Veterans under the following conditions:

1. A $12,480 dollar deduction is available to veterans who:

    a. Served at least 90 days of honorable service.
       And:

    b. Are totally disabled (not necessarily service-connected but the disability must be evidenced by a U.S. Department of Veterans Affairs pension certificate).
       Or:

    c. Are at least 62 years old and 10% service-connected disabled.

Note: This deduction is not available if the assessed value of the real property owned by the veteran is in excess of $113,000.

1. A $24,960tax deduction is available for veterans who:

    a. Served honorably in the Armed Forces during any period of wartime.
       And:

    b. Are at least 10% service-connected disabled.

2. A $37,440 tax deduction is available for any veteran who:

a. a. Served honorably during any period of wartime. And:

b. b. Is 100% service connected-disabled. Or:

c. c. Is at least 62 years of age with at least a 10% service-connected disability.

Indiana Employment Benefits

Employment Assistance
With funding from the U.S. Department of Labor, Veterans' Employment and Training Service, the Indiana Department of Workforce Development provides services to Hoosier Veterans. Through the Disabled Veterans' Outreach Program (DVOP), and the Local Veterans' Employment Representative (LVER) Program, Workforce Development Offices throughout the State are equipped to assist Hoosier Veterans with their transition from the service to civilian life. The DVOPs specialize in tailored training and job placement opportunities for veterans with service-connected disabilities. LVERs coordinate services provided veterans including counseling, testing, and identifying training and employment opportunities.

Indiana Education Benefits

High School Diploma Program for WWI and WWII Veterans
Veterans who served between April 6, 1917 and November 11, 1918 (World War I), or December 7, 1941 and December 31, 1946 (World War II) may apply to the Indiana Department of Veterans' Affairs for issuance of an high school diploma. Veterans must have:

- attended public or nonpublic high school in Indiana prior to military service
- been a student in good standing
- not graduated or received a diploma because of leaving high school for military service
- and, been honorably discharged from the armed forces of the United States

Veterans, or their surviving spouses or eligible family members, may submit application to the Department of Veteran Affairs.

Remission of Fees (Free Tuition) for the Child(ren) of a Disabled Veteran
The natural or legally adopted child(ren) of a disabled veteran may be eligible for remission of fees (free tuition) at any state-supported post secondary school or university in the State of Indiana. This applies at any age as long as the child was adopted by age 24 and the child is a resident of Indiana.

The Remission of Fees is good for 124 semester hours of education and may be used for either undergraduate or graduate level work. The amount remitted is 100% of tuition and all mandatory fees. The term "mandatory fees" is defined as any fee that must be paid by every student attending the institution.

Other Indiana State Veteran Benefits

County Veterans Service Officers

Ninety-one counties in the State employ a County Veterans Service Officer (CVSO). These CVSO's are veterans who stand ready to help you with your veteran-related needs. The County Veterans Service Offices have all the forms and other information you may need to obtain service from the U. S. Department of Veterans Affairs. The Service Officers will assist you in finding the information and resources you need to solve your service-related problems. They are your liaison for all veteran issues.

Golden Hoosier Passport
A Hoosier Golden Passport provides unlimited admission to all Indiana State owned parks, recreation areas, reservoirs, forests, historic sites, museums, memorials and other Department of Natural Resource (DNR) facilities. The pass is good for one calendar year.

Persons eligible for a Disabled American Veteran license plate under IC 9-18-18-1 may purchase the Hoosier Golden Passport at DNR facilities around the State. If you have Disabled American Veteran plates on the vehicle simply drive to the gate and the attendant will sell you the Hoosier Golden Passport. If you do not have the plate but believe you are eligible you will be given a form to request the plate, which you must send to the Indiana Department of Veterans Affairs for verification.

Indiana Veterans Memorial Cemetery
The Indiana Veterans Memorial Cemetery opened for internments on December 1, 1999. The Cemetery is located adjacent to the Madison State Hospital and Clifty Falls State Park in Madison, Indiana. Any Hoosier veteran eligible to be buried in a national cemetery will be eligible for burial in the Cemetery. The spouse of an eligible veteran will also be eligible to be buried there. For an application for burial contact the Indiana Department of Veterans Affairs.

Burial allowances: Each County Auditor is authorized to pay up to an amount not to exceed $100 for the burial of a veteran or the veteran's spouse, and to pay up to $100 for the setting of a federal headstone. Veterans must have received an honorable discharge, and an application must be filed with the county auditor in the county of residence.

Motor Vehicle License Plates
Indiana currently has the following license plates available to eligible veterans:
Hoosier Veteran Plates: Any resident of the State who was honorably separated from the active Armed Forces can purchase a Hoosier Veteran license plate. Simply take your DD-214 or your Discharge Certificate to your local BMV office and request the special plate. There is a $15 charge for the Hoosier Veteran plate.

Disabled Veteran Plates: Disabled Veteran plates are the same as handicap plates in the State of Indiana. These are strictly limited to those individuals who have a serious mobility impairment due to a service-connected disability. Applications may be obtained from either the BMV or the Indiana Department of Veterans Affairs. The Indiana Department of Veterans Affairs must verify the veteran's eligibility.

Ex-Prisoner of War Plates: The POW license plate is available to all ex-prisoners of war or to the surviving spouse of a deceased POW. Applications for these plates are available from the Indiana Department of Veterans Affairs. The Indiana Department of Veterans Affairs must verify the eligibility of the applicant.

Purple Heart Plates: Any Hoosier Veteran who has received the Purple Heart Medal is authorized to have these special license plates. Applications may be obtained at the BMV or from the Indiana Department of Veterans Affairs. The veteran must present official documentation of the award, and the Indiana Department of Veterans Affairs must verify the veteran's eligibility.

All plates may be purchased through the mail or at your local license branch. All plates except the Hoosier Veteran plate must be applied for through the Indiana Department of Veterans Affairs. The Hoosier Veteran plate does not require the completion of an application form, as do the other veteran plates. For more information on each plate, see eligibility for veteran license plates.

Peddlers, Vendors, or Hawkers License
State law provides that any wartime veteran who has an honorable discharge shall be granted these licenses by all cities and counties free of charge. See your county auditor.

Resident Veteran Hunting and Fishing License
Any Indiana resident who is service-connected disabled by the U.S. Department of Veterans Affairs may purchase a license to hunt and fish in the State of Indiana for a reduced fee.

In order to receive this benefit the veteran must complete the Application for Reduced Fee Hunting and Fishing License for Disabled Veterans available from County Veteran Service Officers, from the Department of Natural Resource offices, or from the Indiana Department of Veterans Affairs. The form verifies that the veteran is service-connected disabled and authorizes the reduced fee and is verified by the Indiana Department of Veterans Affairs.

Vital Documents For Veterans Benefits
The Indiana Department of Veterans Affairs and the Indiana State Archives have copies of DD-214's on file for many Hoosier Veterans who entered the service from Indiana. Copies of these will be provided upon request to the Indiana Department of Veterans Affairs. The processing time for such a request is usually one or two weeks. The Indiana Department of Veterans Affairs or your County Veterans Service Officer can assist you with the paperwork to obtain other documents from the federal government.

Iowa State Veteran's Benefits

The state of Iowa provides several veteran benefits. This section offers a brief description of each of the following benefits.

- Housing Benefits
- Financial Assistance Benefits
- Education Benefits
- Other State Veteran Benefits

Iowa State Benefits Update!

The State of Iowa has new benefits for Veterans:

The Iowa Veteran's Housing Grant Program gives a $5,000 matching grant to any veteran for the purchase of a home, tax free. To qualify, the service member must have served on active duty under title 10, 90 days or more after 9-11-2001. Active duty for training does not count. For more information, log onto www.ifahome.com Veterans also receive an annual property tax exemption on their homes.

The State of Iowa also provides a program called the Injured Veteran Grant Program. The State of Iowa provides grants to any Iowa veteran injured in a combat zone while in the line of duty. The injury does not have to be combat action related. To qualify, the injured veteran must be medically evacuated from a combat zone. Within one week of evacuation, the veteran or his/her designated family member receives a check in the amount of $2,500. The veteran will continue to receive $2,500 every 30 days while he or she is receiving medical treatment, up to a maximum of $10,000. This grant is provided by the state to help off set the additional financial burdens veterans and their families incur during convalescence.

If you join the Iowa National Guard, the State of Iowa will pay 100% of your college tuition for four years, up to a maximum of what the state universities cost. At the current rate, that's about $6,000 a year. This amount can be applied to attend any private or independent college as well. Guardsmen can then use their GI bill to pay for other expenses.

Iowa Veteran Housing Programs

Iowa Veterans Home
Presently, the home provides personalized medical, nursing, rehabilitative care, mental health, pharmacy and dietary services, along with many other services. All the services help make the lives of residents engaged and fulfilling.

Homeownership Assistance
This grant is available to a service member who is buying a home in the state of Iowa. Members must have served on active duty on or after September 11, 2001 and purchased a home after March 10, 2005.

Property Tax Exemption
This benefit reduces a veteran?s assessed home value for property tax purposes by $1,850. In order to qualify, a service member must have served on active duty during a period of war or for a minimum of 18 months during peacetime.

Iowa Financial Assistance Benefits

Injured Veterans Grant Program
Senate File 2312 enacting the injured veterans grant program, which is retroactively applicable to veterans injured after September 11, 2001. A total of $1 million has been

appropriated to the Iowa Department of Veterans Affairs (IDVA) to fund this program. The purpose and legislative intent of this program is to provide immediate financial assistance to the veteran so that family members may be with the veteran during recovery and rehabilitation from an injury or illness received in the line of duty in a combat zone or in a designated hostile fire zone. Since the program is retroactive, it is also intended to reimburse veterans injured after September 11, 2001.

Veterans Trust Fund
The State of Iowa has established a $5 million fund to provide certain services to veterans. Beginning in December 2007, interest from this fund has been available to provide relief for Iowa veterans and their families. Funds can be used for travel expenses for service-related medical care; unemployment or underemployment assistance due to service-related causes, job training, or tuition assistance; assistance with vision, hearing, dental care, durable medical equipment, and prescription drugs; counseling and substance abuse services; emergency vehicle and housing repair; transitional housing in an emergency; emergency room and ambulance transportation assistance; funding to determine whether a deceased veteran is the father or mother of a child; funding for family support groups; and grants for providing honor guard services at veteran's funerals. Trust fund expenditures are approved through the Iowa Veterans Commission.

Iowa Education Benefits

War Orphans Educational Aid
War Orphans Educational Aid may be used to defray the expenses of tuition, matriculation, laboratory and similar fees, books and supplies, board, lodging, and any other reasonably necessary expense for the War Orphan to attend the educational institution of higher learning. Aid is limited to $600.

Operation Recognition High School Diploma
This program furnishes an honorary high school diploma to qualifying veterans who did not complete high school due to armed service enlistment. The application form is used by the IDVA and the Department of Education to establish eligibility for honorably discharged veterans.

Other Iowa State Veteran Benefits

Licenses Plates
Honorably discharged veterans are eligible to purchase specialty veteran license plates for their vehicle. These special plates are available for an additional charge through the Iowa Department of Transportation.

Vietnam Conflict Bonus
Iowa residents who served on active duty for at least 120 days between July 1, 1973 and May 31, 1975 are eligible for this bonus program. Veterans who served in Vietnam will receive $17.50 for each month served. Veterans that served outside of Vietnam during this time will receive $12.50 for each month of service. The maximum bonus amount is $500 for veterans who served in Vietnam and $300 for those who were not in country.

Veteran Lifetime Hunting/Fishing License

Veterans in receipt of at a 0% service connected disability can receive a lifetime hunting or fishing license for a $5.50 fee. In order to qualify, the Iowa resident must have served on active federal service and was disabled as a result of that service.

The State of Iowa Veterans Cemetery
The Iowa Veterans Cemetery began operation on July 3, 2008. Located 10 miles west of Des Moines, near Van Meter, the cemetery is available to all veterans, their spouses, and dependent children for burial. Honorably discharged veterans will be interred at no charge and spouses/dependents will be buried for a $300 fee.

Kansas State Veteran's Benefits

The state of Kansas provides several veteran benefits. This section offers a brief description of each of the following benefits.

- Veteran Housing Benefits
- Financial Assistance Benefits
- Employment Benefits
- Education Benefits
- Other State Veteran Benefits

Kansas Veteran Housing Programs

Home Loans
The State of Kansas can assistance in locating approved lenders and completing applications for loan guarantees.

The VA and local banks offer a number of home loan services to eligible veterans, some military personnel, and certain spouses.VA can guarantee part of a loan from a private lender to help you buy a home, a manufactured home, a lot for a manufactured home, or certain types of condominiums. The VA also guarantees loans for building, repairing, and improving homes. VA mortgage, the VA can help you refinance your loan at a lower interest rate. You may also refinance a non-VA loan.

Kansas Financial Assistance Benefits

Dependents' and Survivors' Benefits
Dependency and Indemnity Compensation (DIC) is payable to certain survivors of:VA disability compensation at time of death.

Disability Benefits
Disability Compensation: The KCVA can assist you in filing the forms for Disability Compensation for service connected disability determinations.

Disability Pension: The KCVA can assist you in filing the necessary forms for Disability Pension.

Burial Benefits

Headstones and Markers: The State of Kansas can furnish a monument to mark the unmarked grave of an eligible veteran if not covered by the federal government.

Presidential Memorial Certificate (PMC): The State of Kansas can complete a request to provide a PMC for eligible recipients.

Burial Flag: The United States Post Office or the State of Kansas through the Kansas Veterans' Affairs Commission can provide an American flag to drape over an eligible veteran's casket.

Reimbursement of Burial Expenses: The State of Kansas can assist in completing the forms necessary to receive a burial allowance of $2,000 for veterans who die of service-related causes. For certain other veterans, the VA can pay $300 for burial and funeral expenses and $300 for a burial plot.

Burial in a National or State Veterans Cemetery: Most veterans, spouses and some dependents can be buried in a national cemetery or one of the three state veterans cemeteries at no cost to the veteran or their family.

Time Limits: There is no time limit for claiming reimbursement of burial expenses for a service-related death. In other cases, claims must be filed within 2 years of the veteran's burial.

Prescription Drug Coverage

The State of Kansas can assist in completing the application process to determine eligibility for VA provided medications for certain high priority veterans, including those with low incomes (below VA pension thresholds). Eligible veterans can receive free prescriptions or may be eligible for medications with a low co-payment.

- Service members who died on active duty
- Veterans who died from service-related disabilities
- Certain veterans who were being paid 100%

The State of Kansas can assist you in completing these eligibility forms.

Death Pension is payable to some surviving spouses and children of deceased wartime veterans. The benefit is based on financial need.

- Basic entitlement for a veteran exists if the veteran is disabled as the result of a personal injury or disease (including aggravation of a condition existing prior to service) while in active service if the injury or the disease was incurred or aggravated in line of duty.

Time Limits: There is no deadline for applying for disability benefits.

Kansas Employment Benefits

Vocational Rehabilitation & Employment
The State of Kansas, through the Department of Commerce, can help veterans with service-connected disabilities prepare for, find and keep suitable employment.
The State of Kansas through the Kansas Commission on Veterans' Affairs can assist veterans with serious service-connected disabilities in applying through the VA for services to improve their ability to live as independently as possible. Some of the services provided are:VA notifies you in writing that you have at least a 10 percent rating for a service-connected disability.

- Job Search: Assistance in finding and maintaining suitable employment
- Vocational Evaluation: An evaluation of abilities, skills, interests, and needs
- Career Exploration: Vocational counseling and planning
- Vocational Training: If needed, training such as on-the-job and non-paid work experience
- Education Training: If needed, education training to accomplish the rehabilitation goal
- Rehabilitation Service: Supportive rehabilitation and counseling services

Time Limits: You generally have 12 years

Kansas Education Benefits

Education and Training
Benefits to eligible veterans, dependents, reservists, and service members while they are in an approved training program to include approved university, high school, on the job training and apprenticeship. The State of Kansas can assist you in applying for and approving your participation in these major programs:

- Montgomery GI Bill: Persons who first entered active duty after June 30, 1985, are generally eligible. Some Vietnam Era veterans and certain veterans separated under special programs are also eligible. The bill also includes a program for certain reservists and National Guard members.
- Veterans Educational Assistance Program (VEAP): This program is for veterans who entered active duty for the first time after December 31, 1976, and before July 1, 1985, and contributed funds to this program.
- Kansas National Guard scholarships: available for people who desire a commission in the National Guard.
- Survivors' & Dependents' Educational Assistance: Some family members of disabled or deceased veterans are eligible for education benefits.

Time Limits: Generally, veterans have 10 years from the date they were last released from active duty to use their education benefits. Reservists generally have 10 years from the date they became eligible for the program unless they leave the Selected Reserves before completing their obligation. Spouses generally have 10 years from the date the VA first determines them eligible. Children are generally eligible from age 18 until age 26. These time limits can sometimes be extended.

Other Kansas State Veteran Benefits

Health Care
The State of Kansas can assist you in becoming eligible for the following services:

- Hospital, outpatient medical, dental, pharmacy and prosthetic services
- Domiciliary, nursing home, and community-based residential care including two state veterans' homes offering both domiciliary and nursing home care available to veterans and dependents
- Sexual trauma counseling
- Specialized health care for women veterans
- Health and rehabilitation programs for homeless veterans
- Readjustment counseling
- Alcohol and drug dependency treatment
- Medical evaluation for military service exposure, including Gulf War, Agent Orange, radiation, or other environmental hazards

Filing Claims
In order for benefits of any type to be paid, appropriate claim form(s) must be filed with the VA. Assistance is provided through the KCVA in completing these forms and obtaining supporting records and documents to include military medical records, marriage certificates, death certificates, birth certificates, etc. at no cost to the veteran.

Appealing Claims
Veterans and other claimants for VA benefits have the right to appeal decisions made by a VA regional office. The KCVA in partnership with national service organizations like the American Legion, Disabled American Veterans and the Veteran's of Foreign Wars represent veterans throughout the appeals process.

Medals
The State of Kansas provides assistance to veterans in applying for service medals listed on their DD Form 214.

DD Form 214 (Certificate of Release or Discharge from Active Duty)
The State of Kansas maintains DD Form 214 files on veterans released from service and showing Kansas as their home of record. Copies of DD Form 214's from 1988 to Present may be immediately available in the Kansas Commission on Veterans Affairs central office. The State of Kansas' Adjutant General's Department has an Archives Office, (785) 274-1099, which can provide the following records of service: From 1946 to 1991, DD Form 214's for all branches of the service are available; a Statement of Service on World War II, 1941 -1946; and Kansas National Guard records from 1946 to the present. As required by the Privacy Act and to obtain a copy of DD Form 214, a formal request must be submitted to the Kansas Army National Guard by using Standard Form 180. The State's Kansas State Historical Society, has military records which include some of the following:

- Territorial

- Civil War
- Indian Campaigns
- Spanish American War
- World War I and II

Kentucky State Veteran's Benefits

The state of Kentucky provides several veteran benefits. This section offers a brief description of each of the following benefits.

- Housing Benefits
- Financial Assistance Benefits
- Employment Assistance
- Education Benefits
- Other State Veteran Benefits

Kentucky Veteran Housing Programs

State Veterans Long Term Care Facilities
The Commonwealth of Kentucky is committed to providing long-term care facilities for Kentucky's veterans, offering a broad range of versatile nursing care.

Each of Kentucky's three facilities has a compassionate and professional staff committed to providing thoughtful, quality care. These facilities are also fully prepared to provide care for dementia and Alzheimer residents. Additionally, each of our homes are outfitted with state of the art equipment. Physical therapy and recreational activities are available to help our residents achieve their ultimate functioning abilities.

Learn more about the State Veterans Long Term Care Facilities

Kentucky Financial Assistance Benefits

New Military Family Assistance Trust Fund
Kentucky has introduced a new Military Family Assistance Trust Fund to provide assistance to all Kentucky Home of Record military members and dependents who are facing undue hardships caused by deployments outside of the United States.

Contact your nearest Kentucky Dept. of Veterans' Affairs Representative for more information.

Veterans Loan Program
KDVA has a program to offer small sum loans to Kentucky Veterans, however, this program cannot begin until KDVA designs the program and gets approval for regulation on how the program will operate. KDVA hopes to launch the program soon, and will keep veterans informed about the program through their email distribution lists and press releases

to the media.

Employment Assistance

KDVA and the Kentucky Personnel Cabinet work together to ensure that veterans are able to take full advantage of the state employment opportunities available to them. The Veterans Liaison at Personnel helps veterans to identify jobs appropriate for them and compose applications that fully explore the skills they learned in the military.

State Employment Preference Points

Kentucky offers state employment preference points for veterans, their Spouses, widows, widowers, and parents. The program provides 5 hiring preference points for honorably discharged veterans and for former members of the Kentucky National Guard. 10 points are awarded to veterans with service-connected disabilities and certain spouses of veterans with service-connected disabilities. Surviving spouses of certain war veterans and parents who were dependent on a veteran who lost his/her life under honorable conditions while on active duty are also also entitled to 10 preference points. (Preference points are credited towards state employment when testing at the Personnel Cabinet in Frankfort.)

Kentucky Education Benefits

Tuition Waiver Program
A waiver of tuition is an education benefit provided by the Commonwealth of Kentucky in recognition of military service of certain Kentucky veterans. The tuition waiver is provided for children, stepchildren, adopted children, spouses, and unremarried widows & widowers. An approved tuition waiver means a student may attend any two-year, four-years schools or vocational technical schools that are operated and funded by the Kentucky Department of Education.

You may qualify if one of the following is true of the veteran:

- Died on active duty.
- Died as a direct result of a service connected disability as determined by the U.S. Department of Veterans Affairs.
- 100% service connected disabled.
- Totally disabled (non-service connected) with wartime service.
- Upon the death of any veteran who served during a wartime period.

Other Kentucky State Veteran Benefits

Homeless Veterans Program
We are working to ensure the homeless provider network here in Kentucky is aware that most homeless veterans are eligible for VA benefits and their needs differ from the non-veteran homeless community. We have been able to network around the state and assess the variety of programs or lack of programs offered. KDVA has partnered with Volunteers of America (VOA) to operate a drug/alcohol treatment/transitional housing program at the Lexington, Kentucky VAMC (Leestown Campus). The 40-bed program began enrolling veterans in on

April 8, 2005. KDVA will have a presence at the facility to assist those veterans in their claims.

Women Veterans Program
The mission of the program is to ensure Kentucky?s women veterans have equitable access to federal and state veterans' services and benefits. The program provides assistance to women who served in the United States Armed Forces or in forces incorporated as part of the United States Armed Forces and who were discharged under conditions other than dishonorable. The Women Veterans Coordinator for the Commonwealth collaborates with federal, state, and local agencies on issues related to women veterans; performs outreach to improve awareness of eligibility for services and benefits; assesses the needs of women veterans with respect to benefits and services; makes recommendations to the commissioner to improve benefits and services; and incorporates women veterans' issues in strategic planning concerning benefits and services.

Veteran Designation on Driver's License
The 2012 General Assembly, through enactment of House Bill 221, authorized a special veteran designation on driver's licenses. The word "VETERAN" will be printed vertically and in capital letters along the right border of the license holder's photo. To obtain a license with the designation, a veteran must present a DD214 – the Department of Defense form that verifies service – at the office of the local circuit court clerk, where driver's licenses are issued.

Burial Honors
KDVA helps implement and assist Veterans Service Organizations with Burial Honors Programs. Any Veterans Service Organization seeking a stipend for providing honors should contact our Burial Honors Program Coordinator, (888) 724-7683. Certification of Veterans Service Organizations performing Burial Honors by the National Guard, Ft. Knox or Ft. Campbell has been suspended as a result of operational requirements brought about by current world events.

State Veterans Cemeteries
Kentucky Veterans Cemeteries are located in Hopkinsville, Kentucky, Fort Knox, Williamstown, Greenup County and soon in Leslie County.

Louisiana State Veteran's Benefits

The state of Louisiana provides several veteran benefits. This section offers a brief description of each of the following benefits.

- Housing Benefits
- Employment Benefits
- Education Benefits
- Other State Veteran Benefits

Louisiana Veteran Housing Programs

Louisiana War Veterans Homes

The Louisiana Department of Veterans Affairs operates five War Veterans Homes. These homes, located in Reserve, Monroe, Bossier City, Jackson, and Jennings provide nursing care.

For admission to a Louisiana State Veterans Home, a veteran must be a resident of the state of Louisiana. State residence is not mandatory if the applicant is referred from an in-state United States Department of Veterans'Affairs Medical Center or by a Louisiana Department of Veterans' Affairs Veterans' Assistance Counselor. The applicant must agree to abide by all rules and regulations governing the Home. Applicants who have income will be expected to pay for their care as is set forth in the care and maintenance schedule adopted for governing the Home residents. The applicant must undergo an examination to ascertain whether he/she meets the criteria for admission to the Home.

Please view this list of Admission Requirements or call toll free 1-877-432-8982.

Louisiana Employment Benefits

Military Service Relief Act
Revised Statutes 29:401-425 relative to military and veterans affairs provide for employers compensation, leave status, retirement credit, life, health and accident insurance coverage, re-employment rights upon release from military service, prohibits against academic penalties, deferral of state income taxes, validation of professional and occupational licenses, and protection of any vacancy in office held by an Elected or Appointed Official, for citizens of Louisiana called to military service in the reserve components of the Armed Forces of the United States. The district court in which the state or its political subdivision exercises authority or conducts its business shall have jurisdiction to hear action to enforce the Act.

Veterans Civil Service Preference (Employment Preference)
Article X, of the Louisiana Constitution provides a five-point preference in original appointments to persons honorably discharged from the Armed Forces of the United States who served between the following dates of wartime service:

April 6, 1917, through November 11, 1918
September 27, 1940, through July 25, 1947
June 25 1950, through January 31, 1955
July 1, 1958, through May 7, 1975
August 2, 1990, through, date to be determined
(must have been awarded the Southwest Asia Medal)
Or in a peacetime campaign or expedition if a campaign badge or expeditionary medal is authorized.

Ten points preference in original appointments are accorded each honorable discharged veteran who served in either war or peacetime and has one or more service connected disabilities established with the U.S. Department of Veterans Affairs.

Veterans preference also extends to layoffs over other employees of equal lengths of service and efficiency ratings.

Louisiana Education Benefits

Dependents Educational Assistance
Section 288 of Title 29 of the Louisiana Revised Statutes of 1950 has been amended and re-enacted to provide financial aid for children and surviving spouses of certain veterans of this state who died in service in the Armed Forces of the United States or died of a service connected disability incurred during a wartime period.

The law provides the same benefits for those children of living veterans who are rated 90% or above disabled, including 100% individual unemployability, by the U.S. Department of Veterans Affairs "Schedule for Rating Disabilities", as a result of a disability or disabilities incurred in service in the Armed Forces of the United States.

The law further requires that the deceased veteran must have been a resident of the State of Louisiana for at least twelve months immediately preceding entry into service. The living veteran must have resided in the state not less than twenty-four months immediately preceding the child's admission into the Program.

The surviving spouse must use this Program within ten years of the date eligibility is established. A child must be between the ages of sixteen and twenty-five.

National Guard Tuition
The Adjutant General of Louisiana is responsible for the overall policies, guidance, administration, and proper utilization of this program.

Veterans Education and Training - State Approving Agency
Congress passed the legislation for Chapter 36 of Title 38 U.S.C. 38. The State Approving Agency's mission is to conduct inspection/approval, supervision and provide technical assistance to those programs of education pursued by veterans and other eligible persons receiving educational benefits under Title 38, U.S. Code and Title 10, U.S. Code Chapter 1606. The goals are to ensure that all programs of education, job training, and flight schools are available to veterans and other eligible persons.

Visit the Louisiana Department of Veterans Affairs website for contact information and benefits assistance.

Other Louisiana State Veteran Benefits

Free Hunting/Fishing Licenses
Act 417 amends and re-enacts Subsection F of Section 104 and Subsection C of Section 333 of Title 56 of the Louisiana Revised Statutes of 1950 to provide disabled veterans classified with a service connected permanent disability, rated 50% or higher and who are Louisiana residents, to be issued licenses to fish and hunt free of charge. The law further provides for free license books, returns, transfer of license and also licenses for scientific or experimental purposes.

The law further provides that persons in the Armed Forces of the United States on active duty, to be given resident privileges. Applications may be obtained and certified by contacting the local Parish Veterans Service Office.

Free Entrance to State Parks
Act 172 of the 1977 Regular Session of the Louisiana Legislature provides that any Louisiana resident who is a veteran of the Armed Forces of the United States and who has suffered the amputation of a limb or who at any time has been awarded an allowance toward the purchase of an automobile by the U.S. Government or any Louisiana resident who is a veteran of the Armed Forces of the United States who, as the result of a service connected disability, has been classified as 50% or more permanently disabled or permanent and total as a result of non-service connected disabilities shall be exempt from paying the day use entrance fee to any Louisiana state park.

Free "Purple Heart" License Plates
Revised Statute 47:463.26 provides for the issuance of a Free License Plate for recipients of the "Purple Heart" medal to be used in lieu of the regular motor vehicle registration plates. The recipient may be issued only one plate and such plate shall not be subject to renewal requirements applicable to regular numbered plates. A written request submitted with proof of receiving the Purple Heart should be sent to the Department of Public Safety. The surviving spouse may retain this plate in the event of the recipients death.

Motor Vehicle - Disabled Veterans - Special License Plates, Exemptions
Subsection B of Section 463 of Title 47 of the Louisiana Revised Statutes of 1950, as amended and re-enacted by Act 263, Section 1 of the Louisiana Legislature, provides for any amputee or blind veteran of World War II or of service on or after June 27, 1950, who is a Louisiana citizen and who received financial assistance from the U.S. Department of Veterans Affairs in the purchase of an automobile under provisions of Public Law 663 of the 79th Congress as amended, or under Public Law 187 of the 82nd Congress to be exempt from payment of any motor vehicle registration or license tax on such automobile thus received and is also exempt from payment of such tax on each subsequent automobile purchased by him as replacement, so long as it is determined by evidence from the U.S. Department of Veterans Affairs that his disability (disabilities) still meet(s) the requirements which were met originally in establishing his eligibility to an automobile. Fifty percent or more service connected disabled veterans are eligible for the free license plate.

Special Prestigious License Plates for Certain Veterans and Retirees
The Louisiana Legislature has authorized the Division of Motor Vehicles to issue prestige license plates to certain Louisiana veterans and retired (military) veterans. These plates will be issued for use on any privately-owned passenger car, pickup truck, or van of the veteran applicant. The cost of these plates are the same as the regular issue. Contact the Office of Motor Vehicles to obtain a detailed list of these prestige plates and the requirements for issuance thereof.

Recording of Discharges
Section 132, Title 44 of the Louisiana Revised Statutes of 1950 provides for, upon presentation of the Discharge Certificate or other evidence, the register of Conveyances shall

record in his records, without charge, each Discharge Certificate or other evidence of honorable separation from the Armed Forces of the United States of men and women who have served in these Forces.

Maine State Veteran's Benefits

The state of Maine provides several veteran benefits. This section offers a brief description of each of the following benefits.

- Housing Benefits
- Financial Assistance Benefits
- Education Benefits
- Other State Veteran Benefits

Maine Veteran Housing Programs

Maine Veterans' Homes
To qualify for admission, the applicant must be an honorably discharged veteran who served on active duty in the United States Armed Forces for no less than 180 days.

Eligible veterans must either be residents of Maine at the time of application, or have resided in Maine at the time of entry into the United States Armed Forces. Spouses, widows, widowers, and gold star parents of eligible veterans may also be eligible for admission. Gold star parents are parents of a son or a daughter killed in the line of duty.

Maine Financial Assistance Benefits

Veterans Small Business Loan Program
To learn about the Veterans Small Business Loan Program, visit the FAME website.

Property Tax Exemption
This bulletin has been prepared in order to outline the complex provisions relating to property tax exemption of veterans. Particular notice should be given to the different classifications of exemption so that the municipality may claim the appropriate reimbursement from the State for taxes lost by reason of such exemption.

Prior to April 1, 1978, municipalities were not reimbursed for property taxes lost due to the granting of veterans exemptions. In 1978, the Constitution was amended to reimburse municipalities not less than 50% of property tax revenue loss because of statutory property tax exemptions enacted after April 1, 1978.

Maine Education Benefits

Veterans Dependents Education Benefits Program
Spouses of veterans who are attending state-supported postsecondary vocational schools or institutions of collegiate grade must be admitted free of tuition including mandatory fees and

lab fees for associate's, bachelor's and master's degree programs. Room and board may not be waived.

Children of veterans who are attending state-supported postsecondary vocational schools or institutions of collegiate grade must be admitted free of tuition including mandatory fees and lab fees for associate's and bachelor's programs. The tuition waiver provided under this paragraph may be reduced by an amount necessary to ensure that the value of this waiver, combined with all other grants and benefits received by the student, does not exceed the total cost of education. Room and board may not be waived.

A child of a veteran has 6 academic years from the date of first entrance to complete 8 semesters. The director may waive the limit of 6 consecutive academic years when the Recipient's education has been interrupted by severe medical disability or illness making continued attendance impossible.

Other Maine State Veteran Benefits

Maine Veterans Memorial Cemetery
The Maine Veterans Memorial Cemetery System consists of three cemeteries. The three cemeteries are contemporary parks of memorial design with all grave markers placed flush with the ground level. By law, the State of Maine holds title to all grave lots. The State will, without charge, open and close the grave and furnish perpetual care.

Recreational Licenses
For information about recreational licenses, visit Maine.gov.

Veteran License Plates
To find Veteran Plates Issued by the Bureau of Motor Vehicles, visit
http://www.maine.gov/sos/bmv/registration/vetplatesavailable.htm.

Benefits Available from the Division of Motor Vehicles
Qualified veterans can get a special veteran plate containing the disability symbol to enable them to park in designated parking spaces. The new plate is an expanded design of the standard "Special Veteran" plate which bears the red "V". This new plate also bears the red "V" on the left hand side of the plate and has the universal disability symbol on the far right. This plate does not replace the current "Disabled Veteran" plate which bears a flag and is available to those veterans who qualify based on a service connected disability.

Maryland State Veteran's Benefits

The state of Maryland provides several veteran benefits. This section offers a brief description of each of the following benefits.

- Housing Benefits
- Financial Assistance Benefits
- Employment Benefits

- Education Benefits
- Health Care
- Other State Veteran Benefits

Maryland Veteran Housing Programs

Charlotte Hall Veterans Home
Maryland's veteran's home is located on 125 acres on the site of the former Charlotte Hall Military Academy in Charlotte Hall, Maryland. Opened in 1985, the 504-bed facility provides a continuum of care from the 226-bed Assisted Living unit to a higher level of care in the 278-bed Nursing Home. Specialized care, for those suffering from Alzheimer's and other related dementia, is provided in a 42-bed secured unit. Listed below are the eligibility requirements:

- Honorably discharged veteran of the United States Armed Forces or the legal spouse of a veteran eligible to be admitted to Charlotte Hall*
- Maryland resident
- Age 62 or older, unless disabled and unable to work

Maryland Financial Assistance Benefits

Property Tax Exemption
A property tax exemption is available to veterans who are permanently and totally disabled from service-connected causes, for their primary residence located in the State of Maryland.

The exemption passes to the veteran's spouse upon his or her death. The surviving spouse of active duty military personnel who died in the line of duty as well as the surviving spouse of a totally disabled veteran, or a spouse who receives the dependency and indemnity compensation (effective June 30, 2006) may also receive an exemption.

Military Retired Pay Income Tax Exemption
Military retirees are exempt from Maryland income tax on the first $5000 of their retirement income. In addition, military retirees who are over the age of 65, totally disabled, or who have a spouse who is totally disabled receive an additional subtraction. (Effective July 31, 2006, for all taxable years after December 31, 2005)

Vessel Excise Tax
Active duty military personnel are exempt from the 5% vessel excise tax levied on the sale, resale or transfer of a vessel. The exemption is for not more than one year to current owners of vessels who are members of the armed services and who are serving on active duty.

Survivor Benefits
The surviving spouse, child, dependent parent, or estate of any Maryland resident who is killed while serving in the uniformed services of the United States in the conflict in Iraq or Afghanistan shall receive a $50,000 death benefit and property tax exemption.

Maryland Employment Benefits

Employment & Business Assistance Programs
Maryland offers several employment assistance help veterans successfully transition to a civilian career. In addition the state offers several programs to help veterans start and run their own small business enterprises.

Maryland Education Benefits

Edward T. Conroy Memorial Scholarship
Aid for tuition and other educational expenses are available for veterans and their family members who are attending an institution of higher learning within the borders of the State of Maryland. You must be:

- A veteran or active duty military member who served in the conflicts in Iraq or Afghanistan (Effective June 1, 2006)

- The son or daughter of a member of the United States Armed Forces who died or was 100 percent disabled as a direct result of military service;

- A veteran who suffers, as a direct result of military service, a disability of 25 percent or greater and has exhausted or is no longer eligible for federal veterans' educational benefits;

- The son, daughter or surviving spouse of a victim of the September 11, 2001 terrorist attack who died as a result of the attacks on the World Trade Center in

- New York City, the attack on the Pentagon in Virginia, or the crash of United Airlines Flight 93 in Pennsylvania;

- A POW/MIA of the Vietnam Conflict or his/her son or daughter; the son, daughter or surviving spouse (who has not remarried) of a state or local public safety employee or volunteer who died in the line of duty;

- Or a state or local public safety employee or volunteer who was 100 percent disabled in the line of duty.

High School Diplomas
County Boards of Education award high school diplomas to Korea and World War II veterans who left high school early to enter the Armed Forces. Diplomas are also issued to any veteran upon successful completion of the General Educational Development (GED) test.

Visit the Maryland Department of Veterans Affairs website for contact information and benefits assistance.

Maryland Veteran Health Care Programs

Veteran Health Care Programs
Maryland offers several health care programs to help both young and older veterans. These programs include mental health assistance, PTSD, and drug and alcohol abuse programs.

Other Maryland State Veteran Benefits

Veterans Benefit Claims Assistance Program
The Service and Benefits Program of the Maryland Department of Veterans Affairs assists veterans and eligible dependents in acquiring their benefits. The staff of the Service Program is authorized to represent veterans and their dependents before the United States Department of Veterans Affairs as well as provide general information to those seeking assistance, regardless of representation.

The Service Program currently has Service Officers located in communities throughout Maryland to aid or serve veterans and their eligible dependents. Contact the Program Office most convenient to you. Appointments may be scheduled through the Program Office nearest the itinerant location.

State Veterans Cemetery & Memorial Program
The Maryland Department of Veterans Affairs administers a system of five state veterans' cemeteries, across the State and oversees the Washington Confederate Cemetery located in the Rose Hill Cemetery. A burial plot is provided to eligible veterans and their eligible dependents, when the veteran is a resident of the State of Maryland and has received an honorable discharge. Plots are available on a first-come, first-served basis. There is no cost to the veteran for burial plot, opening/closing, headstone and State liner (if used). Eligible dependents have a minimal opening/closing cost and a direct cost for State liner (if used). There is also a pre-interment program where veterans can indicate their desire to be buried in one of the Five (5) State veteran's cemeteries and verify their eligibility for burial.

Maryland Veterans Memorials
The Maryland Department of Veterans Affairs manages three veteran memorials. The Maryland World War II Memorial is in Annapolis, Korean War and Maryland Veterans Vietnam Memorials are in Baltimore. The Department shares joint responsibility for the War Memorial Building in Baltimore with the City of Baltimore.

Obtaining Copies of Documents
Whenever a veteran requests benefits and services, a copy of the individual's discharge papers is required to verify eligibility. This includes admission to Charlotte Hall Veterans Home, Maryland's five veteran cemeteries, VA claims and a myriad of other services provided to veterans and their families. World War II veterans who were Maryland residents at the time of entry into the service, and veterans who were discharged after October 15, 1979 and had a Maryland address at the time of discharge, can contact our Baltimore Office to inquire if we have a copy of their discharge papers. Veterans and their next of kin can also request a copy of the service member's DD Form 214, Certificate of Release or Discharge from Active Duty from the National Archives.

Game Hunting & Fishing Licenses
100% service-connected disabled veterans and former POWs may obtain free hunting and fishing licenses. Additionally, Maryland residents in the Armed Forces, or service members who are on active duty and stationed in Maryland, may hunt without cost, if they are on official leave.

Admission to State Parks
The Maryland Park Service offers an Access MD Pass for free entry to State Parks to individuals with disabilities. Additionally, the Golden Age Pass allows free entry to individuals

62 and older.

Auto Tags
Certain severely disabled veterans (amputees, blind veterans and veterans who are 100% disabled) may be issued a disabled license plate for a motor vehicle without charge entitling them to special parking privileges.

Massachusetts State Veteran's Benefits

The state of Massachusetts provides several veteran benefits. This section offers a brief description of each of the following benefits.

- Housing Benefits
- Financial Assistance Benefits
- Education Benefits
- Recently-Returned Combat Veterans
- Other State Veteran Benefits

Massachusetts Veteran Housing Programs

Public Assistance
Under Chapter 115 of Massachusetts General Laws, the Commonwealth provides a uniform program of financial and medical assistance for indigent veterans and their dependents.

Qualifying veterans and their dependents receive necessary financial assistance for food, shelter, clothing, housing supplies, and medical care in accordance with a formula which takes into account the number of dependants and income from all sources. Eligible dependents of deceased veterans are provided with the same benefits as they would were the veteran still living.

Massachusetts Financial Assistance Benefits

Tax Exemptions
Property Tax: Eligible veterans, spouses, and parents. To qualify, all veterans (and spouses* where applicable) must:

- be at least 10% disabled by the U.S. Department of Veterans Affairs
- be legal residents of Massachusetts
- be occupying the property as his/her domicile on July 1 in the year of application
- have lived in Massachusetts for at least six months prior to entering the service (spouses exempted) or
- have lived in Massachusetts for five consecutive years immediately prior to filing for a property tax exemption.

Motor Vehicle Tax:

Disabled veterans of World War I, World War II, Korea, or Vietnam who by reason of service in the U.S. armed forces have suffered the loss of, or permanent loss of the use of, one or both feet or one or both hands or the loss of sight in one eye or who have permanent impairment of vision of both eyes (see statute for details) and are certified by the U.S. Department of Veterans Affairs are eligible for motor vehicle excise exemption (applicable only to one motor vehicle owned and registered for personal, non-commercial use).

Sales Tax Exemption for Disabled Veterans:

Disabled veterans who by reason of service in the U.S. armed forces have suffered the loss of, or permanent loss of the use of, both legs or both arms or one leg and one arm are eligible for a motor vehicle sales tax exemption (applicable only to one motor vehicle owned and registered for personal, non-commercial use).

Annuities
An annuity in the amount of $2000, which is payable biannually on August 1st and February 1st in two installments of $1000 each is available for certain veterans and their spouses, as well as Gold Star Parents. This benefit is provided by the Commonwealth of Massachusetts, through the Department of Veterans' Services.

Bonuses
The Commonwealth of Massachusetts provides a bonus to veterans who were domiciled in Massachusetts immediately prior to entry in the armed forces. In case of the death of a veteran, the spouse and children, mother or father, brother or sister or other dependents of the deceased veteran (in that order) are eligible for a bonus.

- World War II Bonus
- Korean War Bonus
- Vietnam War Bonus
- Persian Gulf War Bonus
- Welcome Home Bonus

Massachusetts Education Benefits

Education Financial Assistance
Tuition Waivers: A Tuition waiver for all Massachusetts veterans to all state colleges and universities

Veterans of Massachusetts can be eligible for a tuition waiver at any state-supported course in an undergraduate degree program offered by a public college or university. To be eligible, a veteran must also be a legal resident of Massachusetts and he/she must not be in default of any federal student loans.

Veterans will be eligible on a space-available basis for a waiver of full or partial tuition based on proper documentation of the eligibility of the veteran. Space availability shall be determined in accordance with normal practices and procedures as published by each institution, i.e., the individual college or university.

Tuition and Fee Waivers for Guard Members: Tuition and fee waiver for members of the

Massachusetts National Guard at all state colleges and universities

The Massachusetts National Guard Education Assistance Program provides a 100% tuition and fee waiver for Massachusetts National Guard soldiers attending a state college, university, or community college program. Generally, these state-supported programs are offered during the day as part of a degree program. Your assistance can continue as long as you are in good standing academically and until you have reached 130 semester hours.

Massachusetts Public Service Grant Program: The Massachusetts Public Service Grant Program was established in recognition of the hardship that a family experiences upon the loss of a parent and or spouse who is killed or missing in the line of public service duty in the Commonwealth of Massachusetts. This grant program was established to provide educational opportunity to the remaining family members. The Public Service Grant Program is the only scholarship program not based on demonstrated financial need, but rather entitlement.

Deployed Troops Get Break on Student Loans: Service members who have been deployed or mobilized are not required to make certain student loan payments during their absences. This applies to members of the National Guard and Ready Reserves who have been called to active duty, as well as to active duty members who duty station has been changed as a result of a military mobilization. The regulations apply to students loans made under the Federal Family Education Loan, William D. Ford Federal Direct Loan and Federal Perkins Loan programs. Active duty members who have not begun the repayment period on their loans should continue to receive a grace period (generally six months) before repaying their loans. Students who were in school at the time of mobilization must also be given a reasonable period to resume school before lenders request payments.

Upward Bound Program
The Veterans Upward Bound (VUB) Program at the University of Massachusetts Boston provides a unique opportunity for veterans of all ages to gain access to information about college and career awareness, acquire the academic skills required for entry into higher education and/or to acquire the equivalent of a high school diploma. Services are offered continuously with various workshops, self-paced computer tutorials, individualized tutoring and classroom-based instruction. All Veterans Upward Bound classes and supplies are FREE to qualified veterans.

Eligibility: Must have served at least 181 days of active duty military service.
Discharge must have been other than dishonorable. Low income and first generation college attendance. (You may also be eligible if you meet all the former requirements and are solely low income or solely a first generation college student. Academic need.

Operation Recognition
The Welcome Home Bill (signed November 11, 2005) allows high schools to award diplomas to World War II, Korean, and Vietnam veterans who left school for good upon being drafted or enlisting in the military.

Special Commission to Study Higher Education Tuition & Fee Waivers for Veterans
In November 2005, the Legislature enacted "The Welcome Home Bill," an act providing

benefits to servicemembers, veterans, and their families. The new law provides for many benefits including a waiver of tuition and fees for all members of the Massachusetts National Guard who chose to attend state institutions of higher education. Section 12 of the "The Welcome Home Bill" also created a Special Commission to "study tuition and fee waiver programs'for veterans."

Massachusetts Recently-Returned Combat Veterans

Welcome Home Bonus
You are eligible if you meet the following criteria: six months domicile in Massachusetts immediately prior to entry into the armed forces service, beginning September 11, 2001, and discharge under honorable conditions.

- Servicemembers who served active duty in Iraq or Afghanistan receive $1000.
- Servicemembers with six months or more active service, stateside or outside the continental limits of the United States, receive $500.

Civil Service and Veterans' Preference
If you are a Massachusetts veteran, as defined in the Introduction above, you are entitled to veterans' preference in civil service exams. If you attain a score of 70% or higher, you are entitled to go to the top of the exam list, with disabled veterans having top priority. If you apply for a promotional exam, you get two points added to your score. If you apply for a civil service job for which there is no exam, you are entitled to veterans' preference in a "provisional appointment." If you apply for a position in the labor force, you are not required to take an exam and you go to the top of the list.

Financial and Civil Protections
You have certain financial and civil protections under both federal and state versions of the Soldiers and Sailors Civil Relief Act. These protections occur when you enter military service, and when you are called up for active duty as a member of the Reserve or Guard. Under this law, your protection begins on the date you enter active service, or the date your orders begin, and generally terminates within 30 to 180 days after the date of your discharge depending on the right. To receive some of the protections, you have to be prepared to show that military service has had a "material effect" on the legal or financial matter involved.

Employment Opportunities
There are numerous federal and state programs available to you if you are seeking employment.

VOICE, or Veterans' Outreach Initiative for Competitive Employment, located at the Massachusetts Department of Veterans' Services is a good place to start your search, because they can put you in touch with the various federal and state vocational rehabilitation, career counseling, and job network services located within the Commonwealth.

Education
If you are a veteran, as defined in the Introduction, Massachusetts provides you a full or partial tuition waiver for any state-supported course in an undergraduate degree program or certificate program at the school's discretion. These waivers are also referred to as

"categorical waivers." Call the college or university where you are interested in enrolling and identify yourself as a veteran looking to use the tuition waiver benefit and ask for the veterans' representative. As to tuition waivers for graduate school, it depends on the institution. If you are a member of the Guard, see below for additional tuition waiver benefits.

If you are a member of the Massachusetts Air or Army National Guard you may take advantage of several programs that will allow you to waive tuition at state schools in Massachusetts. The Massachusetts National Guard Education Assistance Program provides a 100% tuition and fee waiver for Massachusetts National Guard soldiers attending a state college, university, or community college program. The fee waiver program is a result of the Welcome Home Bill (HB 4469) signed on November 11, 2005. The fee waiver is not effective until July 2006 and is not retroactive. Generally, these state-supported programs are offered during the day as part of a degree program. Your assistance can continue as long as you are in good standing academically and until you have reached 130 semester hours. Please contact the college or university veteran's representative for details about this program.

Qualifying Guard members can take advantage of another educational program called Federal Tuition Assistance (FTA). The FTA offers $4,500 per fiscal year to be used at regionally or nationally accredited, public or private colleges, universities, vocational, technical, or trade schools located inside or outside the Commonwealth of Massachusetts. The FTA can offer soldiers up to $250 per semester hour for tuition and up to 100% of fees that are charged to all students for enrollment purposes or fees directly related to the instruction of the course. Yes! This means that you can also get help paying for fees at Massachusetts state colleges and universities.

Housing
When you return from active duty, we hope that you know where you will live. Unfortunately some veterans may have lost their housing and are having trouble finding a place to live or having trouble paying the rent or mortgage. The information included below may help you solve your housing problems. If you are having any of these troubles, immediately call or visit the Veterans' Agent in the community where you live or want to live.

The first place to visit is you local Veterans' Agent in the community where you live or want to live. There are also nine state-funded Outreach Centers in every region of the state, which provide help to veterans who are searching for housing. Some Outreach Centers also provide supportive housing for homeless veterans. The VA Medical Centers in Bedford, Boston, Brockton, and Springfield have Homeless Coordinators who can help. Women veterans who are homeless or at-risk for homelessness can get help from the VA Boston's Homeless Women Veterans Outreach and Case Management Program.

Your Local Veterans' Agent
The best place for you to go for help with other questions is to your local Veterans' Agent, who works out of your local City or Town Hall. The Veterans' Agent's job is to help veterans learn about, apply for, and in some cases, receive benefits. Veterans' Agents are knowledgeable about an array of federal, state, and local benefits to which you may be entitled. Your Agent can help you fill out application forms for the benefits listed in this booklet.

Motor Vehicles Benefits
Veteran series license plates, excise tax exemptions, and vehicle registration exemptions are benefits offered to veterans in the Commonwealth of Massachusetts.

Disabled veterans who by reason of service in the U.S. armed forces have suffered the loss of, or permanent loss of, the use of one or both hands or feet, or who have permanent impairment of vision in both eyes, or any other disability or handicap of such veterans that may be determined by the Medical Affairs Branch of the Registry of Motor Vehicles are eligible to receive, free of charge, disabled veterans motor vehicle registration plates and are exempt from the biannual registration renewal fee.

All veterans of any war or military action who, in the course of duty, have been captured and incarcerated by an enemy of the U.S. during an armed conflict are eligible to receive, free of charge, ex-prisoner of war motor vehicle registration plates and are exempt from the biannual registration renewal fee. Presentation of satisfactory evidence of such prisoner of war status is required. A surviving spouse will be able to keep this plate until he/she remarries, or fails to renew or cancels such registration, but an annual fee would then be required.

National Guard & Reserve
Tuition and Fee Waivers for Guard Members: Tuition and fee waiver for members of the Massachusetts National Guard at all state colleges and universities

The Massachusetts National Guard Education Assistance Program provides a 100% tuition and fee waiver for Massachusetts National Guard soldiers attending a state college, university, or community college program. Generally, these state-supported programs are offered during the day as part of a degree program. Your assistance can continue as long as you are in good standing academically and until you have reached 130 semester hours.

Homefront Financial Security Loan Program: In March 2003, State Treasurer Timothy P. Cahill announced a low interest loan program for all resident reservists and Massachusetts National Guard members.

State Benefits for Dependents of a Veteran
The Commonwealth provides a uniform program of financial and medical assistance for indigent veterans and their dependents. Qualifying veterans and their dependents receive necessary financial assistance for food, shelter, clothing, housing supplies, and medical care in accordance with a formula which takes into account the number of dependants and income from all sources. Eligible dependents of deceased veterans are provided with the same benefits as they would were the veteran still living

Michigan State Veterans' Benefits

The state of Michigan provides several veteran benefits. This section offers a brief description of each of the following benefits.

- Housing Benefits
- Education and Financial Assistance Benefits

- Veteran Employment Benefits
- Other State Veteran Benefits

Michigan Veteran Housing Programs

Grand Rapids Home for Veterans
All members of the Armed Forces of the United States who have been honorably discharged and served not less than 90 days during a designated wartime period (i.e., First World War - April 6, 1917, to November 11, 1918, [to April 1920 if served in Russia]; Second World War - December 7, 1941, to December 31, 1946; Korean Conflict, Cold War, Vietnam war - beginning September 2, 1945, through December 26, 1991; or Persian Gulf War August 2, 1990, to present) may apply for admission to said facilities.

D. J. Jacobetti Home for Veterans
The primary mission of the D.J. Jacobetti Home for Veterans is to restore health and maintain existing functions, enabling residents the opportunity to enjoy their remaining years to the fullest.

Keeping pace with the disabled population's changing needs, the D.J. Jacobetti Home for Veterans is a modern nursing home that serves and encourages its veterans to function at their maximum level. The Home's staff places great emphasis on tailoring it's care plans to a member's individual needs and to encourage their independence, rather than dependence. To that end, the Veterans' Home has adopted a comprehensive needs assessment process. Every person admitted to the Home is thoroughly evaluated by a physician, social services, nursing, activities, dietary and physical therapy in terms of abilities and disabilities. This comprehensive assessment results in an "Interdisciplinary Care Plan" issued within the first seven days of admission. An Interdisciplinary Team Meeting is held every 90 days to measure progress. The focus is always on the member's abilities rather than disabilities. A State nursing home operated under the Michigan Department of Military and Veterans Affairs, the D.J. Jacobetti Home for Veterans provides 182 nursing care beds, two infirmary beds and 59 residential beds.

State Veterans Homes Board of Managers
Created by Public Act 152 of 1895, the Board of Managers exercises certain regulatory and governance authority regarding admission and member affairs at Michigan?s two veterans homes. They also represent the interest of the veterans? community in both advisory and advocacy roles. The board members are appointed by the governor, with the advice and consent of the senate, to serve 6-year terms.

Note: Michigan Veterans can find assitsance through their local county veterans services offices. Click here to find the office near you.

Michigan Education and Financial Assistance Benefits

Tuition Grant Procedure Brief
Michigan provides an annual undergraduate tuition grant of up to $2,800 for the eligible

children of certain deceased military personnel or totally and permanently disabled veterans. The Michigan Higher Education Assistance Authority administers the program.

Emergency Grants
Temporary assistance granted by the Michigan Veterans Trust Fund (MVTF) for emergencies or hardships is available to eligible wartime veterans, and their families, residing in the state. Under the authority of Public Act 9 of 1946 (as amended), the MVTF cannot provide assistance for long-term problems or chronic financial difficulties. Those eligible for the MVTF temporary grant program must apply through the MVTF county committee serving their county of residence. All applications are investigated, deliberated, and decided in confidence. Any applicant may request a personal hearing before the county committee at the meeting when his/her application is considered. If the county committee denies an application every applicant has the right to appeal that decision to the MVTF Board of Trustees (with the opportunity to appear before the board to present information and answer questions.) The MVTF does not provide loans under the temporary assistance program.

Michigan National Guard Family Support Funds
For information regarding Michigan National Guard Family Support Funds, visit http://minationalguard.com/familyprograms/family-fund/.

Note: Michigan Veterans can find assistance through their local county veterans services offices.

Michigan Veterans' Employment Services

Michigan offers veterans a large array of employment services including job fairs, career portals and job boards. All can be easily found at the Michigan Veterans Employment Services website.

Visit the Michigan Veterans' Employment website to learn more.

Note: Michigan Veterans can find assitsance through their local county veterans services offices.

Other Michigan State Veterans' Benefits

Michigan Veterans' Programs Booklet
This booklet has been compiled especially for veterans and their families to fulfill three important purposes:
- To provide information concerning veterans benefits and service available through federal, state, and local agencies;
- To provide veterans and their families with links to direct sources, both computer-based and professional, knowledgeable counselors, for answers to specific questions; and
- To assist veterans in communicating more effectively with their elected representatives.

Minnesota State Veteran's Benefits

The state of Minnesota provides several veteran benefits. This section offers a brief description of each of the following benefits.

- Housing Benefits
- Employment Benefits
- Education Benefits
- Other State Veteran Benefits

Minnesota Veteran Housing Programs

Homeless Veterans' Initiative
The Minnesota homeless veterans' initiative and rehabilitation services assist veterans and their families in their attempts to regain self-sufficiency.

Minnesota Veterans' Homes

Minnesota Veterans' Homes are located in Fergus Falls, Hastings, Luverne, Minneapolis and Silver Bay.

Minnesota Employment Benefits

MN Veterans Preference Act
MN Veterans Preference Act (VPA) grants veterans a limited preference over non-veterans in hiring and promotion for MN public employment and also provides protection against unfair dismissals and demotions. VPA grants veterans the right to a hearing, prior to dismissal.

Minnesota Education Benefits

One-Time Educational Grants
Educational benefits are provided in the form of a one-time grant to veterans who have exhausted their federal benefits, and to war orphans of veterans who died as a result of a service connected injury or disease.

Other Minnesota State Veteran Benefits

Services Program
The Department of Veterans Affairs Services Program provides claims representation and fiduciary guardianship services.

Veterans Claims Advocacy
Staff at our Veterans Claims Offices, located at Fort Snelling and at Fargo/Moorhead, act as advocates for veterans and their dependents who are trying to get their benefits from the United States Department of Veterans Affairs (the VA). The staff will assist and represent veterans, their dependents, and survivors with applications for compensation, pension, home loans, educational, and medical treatment. The offices also provide environmental hazards information and assistance (Agent Orange issues, for example). See your County Veterans Service Officer to request this representation.

Guardianship Division
Our Guardianship Division provides financial case management services to incompetent veterans, their dependents, and survivors, who may be vulnerable to exploitation by others or by their own inabilities to manage their funds.

Minnesota State Veterans Cemetery
The Minnesota State Veterans Cemetery provides dignified burial services to Minnesota veterans and their eligible dependents and survivors. It is located 7 miles north of Little Falls, on the banks of the Mississippi River, and is managed and maintained by the Minnesota Department of Veterans Affairs.

Discharge Certificates
Veterans' benefits require that applicants provide a copy of their form DD 214 or discharge record, which is evidence of their veteran status. This is an important document and must be safeguarded. If you do not have a copy of your DD 214, contact your County Veterans Service Officer for assistance in obtaining it. If you have a copy of your DD 214 it is recommended that it be recorded in your county courthouse, or at the very least be sure to keep it in a safe place and inform a family member or trusted individual of its location.

Bronze Star Grave Markers
The Minnesota Department of Veterans Affairs offers bronze stars to mark the grave site of any veteran buried in the state, where permitted. Bronze Star Markers are available through your local county veterans service officer.

Mississippi State Veteran's Benefits

The state of Mississippi provides several veteran benefits. This section offers a brief description of each of the following benefits.

- Housing Benefits
- Financial Assistance Benefits
- Employment Benefits
- Education Benefits
- Other State Veteran Benefits

Mississippi Veteran Housing Programs

Mississippi Veterans Home Purchase Board
The Veterans Home Purchase Board provides low interest mortgage loans for eligible veterans and unmarried surviving spouses to purchase an existing single family home or to construct a new home.

Eligibility requires that the veteran be a Mississippi resident prior to entering military service or be a resident for two (2) consecutive years prior to applying for the loan. The veteran must have or obtain a Certificate of Eligibility for Home Loan Guaranty from the Department of

Veterans Affairs (VA) and be discharged from extended active duty under honorable conditions. The unmarried surviving spouse of eligible persons who died as a result of service or service-connected injuries qualifies, as well as the unremarried spouse of any eligible veteran who has not purchased a home since the veteran?s death are eligible.

State Veterans Nursing Homes
Each of the four State Veterans Nursing Homes have 150 beds and they provide skilled nursing home care for eligible veterans and spouses. Eligibility for admission to the Homes requires that a veteran be or have been a Mississippi resident, have active duty military service, have a "good" military discharge, or be the spouse of a veteran who resides in one of the Veterans Homes. Out of state veterans may be admitted to the Homes if there are no Mississippi residents waiting to accept a bed. Applicants must have a medical need for nursing home care and must be able to pay the daily charge for care in the Home. Applications for admission to the Veterans Homes can be obtained from any of our offices. Indigent veterans can request assistance with the expense of care in the facilities.

Mississippi Financial Assistance Benefits

Privilege Tax
Persons who are 65 or older, blind, deaf, dumb, or with loss of hand or foot, or loss of use of the hand or foot or who can provide documentation that they are 50% disabled to perform physical labor and whose annual gross income is $900.00 or less are exempt from payment of privilege tax for specified businesses.

Ad Valorem Tax
Service-connected, totally disabled (100%) American veterans who were honorably discharged from military service are exempt from all ad valorem taxes on homesteads of $7,500.00 or less in assessed value.

Mississippi Employment Benefits

Re-employment
Any person who is a member of any reserve component of the Armed Forces of the United States who, in order to perform duties or receive training with the Armed Forces of the United States or of the State of Mississippi leaves a position, other than a temporary position, in the employ of any employer, and who shall give evidence of the satisfactory completion of such duty or training, and who is still qualified to perform the duties of such position, shall be entitled to be restored to his previous or a similar position, in the same status, pay, and seniority. Such period of absence for military duty or training shall be construed as an absence with leave but may be without pay.

Employment Preference
The State Personnel Board grants each veteran who is fully qualified preference over other applicants for initial or promotional appointments (5 points). Disabled veterans are given additional preference (10 points). In state layoffs, veterans are granted preference and additional preference is given disabled veterans.

State Retirement
Members of the State Public Employees Retirement System who served in the Armed Forces of the United States or who served in Maritime Service during periods of hostility in WWII shall be entitled to up to four (4) years credit for active duty in the Armed Forces or in such Maritime Service, provided they entered State Service after discharge from the Armed Forces or after completion of such Maritime Service. Credit may be extended beyond four (4) years for those persons who can provide positive proof that they were retained in the Armed Forces or such Maritime Service during WWII by causes beyond his control and without opportunity for discharge.

Mississippi Education Benefits

Educational Assistance
Children of any member of the armed services whose official home of record and residence is within the State of Mississippi and who is officially reported as being either a prisoner of a foreign government or missing in action can receive an eight-semester scholarship, without cost, exclusive of books, food, school supplies, materials and dues or fees for extracurricular activities at any state supported college or university within the State.

The Adjutant General is authorized to pay the tuition for any member in good standing with the active Mississippi National Guard who is enrolled within the State of Mississippi in an accredited institution of higher learning and who is not eligible for GI Bill educational assistance and who meets requirements specified in Mississippi law.

Military personnel stationed in Mississippi are classified as state residents for the purposes of payment of tuition at state colleges and universities.

Mississippi Employment Security Commission
Veterans seeking assistance regarding employment or unemployment insurance benefits should contact their local Mississippi Employment Security Commission Office for assistance. MS Employment Security Commission offices are located in larger cities and towns throughout the state.

Other Mississippi State Veteran Benefits

Documents
The State Bureau of Vital Statistics is to furnish, without charge, copies of birth and death certificates when they are needed to establish claims for dependency, disability, or survivors benefits for any veterans who are legal residents of the State of Mississippi or their claimants.

The State Bureau of Vital Statistics is to furnish, at no expense, and immediately upon application a certified copy of birth certificates for any person volunteering for service in one of the armed forces of the United States.

Chancery and Circuit Clerks are to furnish, without charge, copies of marriage licenses, divorce decrees, adoption decrees and any and all other records when the same are needed to establish claims for dependency, disability or survivors benefits for any veterans who are legal residents of the State of Mississippi or their claimants.

Chancery Clerks shall record, without cost whatsoever to any person of the Armed Forces of the United States residing in the same county, all honorable discharges and all certificates of service of any and all members of the Armed Forces of the United States. Certified copies will be furnished free without cost to the soldier, sailor, marine, coast guardsman, or nurse.

Hunting and Fishing Licenses
Veterans who have a total service-connected disability from the Veterans Administration are not required to purchase a hunting or fishing license, but must have on their person proof of age, residency and disability status while engaged in hunting or fishing.

Vehicle License Plates
The following are special vehicle military license plates issued to eligible persons in Mississippi:

- Medal of Honor
- Disabled American Veteran
- Distinguished Flying Cross & Air Medal
- Former Prisoner of War
- Killed on Active Duty
- Missing in Action - Prisoners of War
- Mississippi Veterans Monument
- Pearl Harbor Survivors
- Purple Heart
- Reserve, National Guard, Merchant Marine, Retired
- Silver Star or Bronze Star Medal
- United States Air Force Academy
- United States Armed Forces Active Duty
- United States Army Special Forces
- United States Coast Guard Academy
- United States Military Academy
- United States Naval Academy
- Veteran
- Vietnam Service

Missouri State Veteran's Benefits

The state of Missouri provides several veteran benefits. This section offers a brief description of each of the following benefits.

- Housing Benefits
- Financial Assistance Benefits

- Employment Benefits
- Other State Veteran Benefits

Missouri Veteran Housing Programs

Missouri Veterans Homes
A current total of seven skilled nursing homes are located throughout Missouri, providing 3 levels of skilled nursing care at minimal cost to the veteran.

Under the management of Missouri Veterans Commission, these homes are located in Cameron, Warrensburg, Mexico, St. Louis, St. James, Cape Girardeau, and Mt. Vernon.

Learn more about Vet Homes at: http://www.mvc.dps.mo.gov/homes/

Missouri Financial Assistance Benefits

Property Tax Credits
If you or your spouse is a 100% service connected disabled veteran, you may qualify for a Property Tax Credit with the State of Missouri. Veterans and non-veterans may also qualify for this credit if they are over age 65 even if they are not 100% disabled.

Tax Exemption for AO Settle Payments
Agent Orange Settlement Payments made for the Agent Orange Fund to a veteran or his dependents are exempt from state tax.

Vietnam Veterans Survivor Grant Program
Legislation passed in 1991 provides that certain surviving widows and children of Vietnam Veterans may qualify to receive tuition-free scholarships to attend institutions of post-secondary education in Missouri. The veteran's death must be attributable to illness that could possibly be a result of exposure to toxic chemicals such as "Agent Orange" during the Vietnam conflict in order for the survivor to qualify. The maximum annual grant amount is the least of: the actual tuition charged at the school in which you are enrolled full time, or the average amount of tuition charged to a Missouri undergraduate resident enrolled full time in the same class level and in the same academic major at the Missouri public four-year, regional institutions.

Missouri Employment Benefits

Veterans' Preference with State of Missouri Employment
Missouri Veterans receive five-point preference when testing for any position with the state, with a ten point preference for a service-connected disabled veteran. Spouses of eligible veterans can also qualify for Veterans Preference for State testing.

Priority for Qualified Veterans Employment
State agencies which administer federally funded employment and training programs for veterans shall give priority to qualified veterans and other eligible persons.

Veterans Service Officers
Located in nearly every county of the state, Veterans Service Officers and Assistants are highly trained individuals who provide counselling and assistance in completing and submitting applications for VA and State Veterans Benefits, as well as any necessary follow-up claimwork. These services are provided free of charge to Missouri's veterans and their dependents.

State Veterans Cemeteries
Missouri Veterans Commission currently operates five State Veterans Cemeteries, one each in Springfield, Higginsville, Bloomfield, Ft. Leonard Wood, and Jacksonville.

World War II, Korean War, and Vietnam War Medals and Medallions
The Veterans Award Program was first established in 2000 with the creation of the World War II Veterans? Award Recognition.

The World War II Veterans? Award Recognition consists of a medal, medallion and certificate. World War II veterans who participated in the D-Day invasion of Europe are also eligible to receive a replica of the Jubilee of Liberty medal.

The Korean War Medallion was added in 2003 and in 2006 the Vietnam War Medallion was added. The Vietnam War award consists of a medal, medallion and Certificate.

Since the program began, over 41,000 Missouri veterans have been awarded the World War II Veterans? Award Recognition.

In the 2003 legislative session, the Korean War Medallion was added. The Korean War award consists of a medal, medallion, and certificate.

Free Automobile License Plates
Veterans who have service-connected disabilities, or in need of adaptive equipment. Disabled Veteran specialty license plates are available to eligible applicants at no fee (limit one set per applicant). To qualify for Disabled Veteran specialty license plates, you must be a Missouri resident who has served in and was honorably discharged from the United States Armed Forces.

In addition, Medal of Honor, Purple Heart recipients, Military Retirees, Former POWs and widows of former POWs qualify for Free Special Automobile License Plates.

Free Fishing & Hunting License
Any honorably discharged resident veteran having a service-related disability of 60% or more, or who was a prisoner of war during military service, may take fish, live bait, clams, mussels, turtles and frogs without permit (except trout permit or daily tag in areas where prescribed), and may take wildlife as provided in Chapter 7 without permit (except deer and turkey hunting permits and the Migratory Bird Hunting Permit as prescribed); provided, while hunting or fishing s/he carries a certified statement of eligibility from the Veterans Administration.

Montana State Veteran's Benefits

The state of Montana provides several veteran benefits. This section offers a brief description of each of the following benefits.

- Housing Benefits
- Financial Assistance Benefits
- Employment Benefits
- Education Benefits
- Other State Veteran Benefits

Montana Veteran Housing Programs

Location and Function of Homes -- Persons Admitted
The institutions at Columbia Falls and in eastern Montana are the Montana veterans' homes, and their primary function is to provide a home and subsistence for veterans.

The department of public health and human services may also admit spouses or surviving spouses of veterans to the homes if space allows.

Certain Disabled or Deceased Veterans' Residences Exempt
A residence, including the lot on which it is built, that is owned and occupied by a veteran or a veteran's spouse is exempt from property taxation if the veteran:

- was killed while on active duty or died as a result of a service-connected disability; or
- if living:
  - was honorably discharged from active service in any branch of the armed services; and
  - is currently rated 100% disabled or is paid at the 100% disabled rate by the U.S. department of veterans affairs for a service-connected disability, as verified by official documentation from the U.S. department of veterans affairs.

Montana Financial Assistance Benefits

Interment Allowance for Veterans
A sum not to exceed $250 to defer interment expenses must be paid by the veteran's county of residence.

The interment benefits are not available in the case of a veteran whose personal representative or heirs waive the benefits.

Whenever interment is of a resident of a Montana veterans' home, a sum not to exceed $250 to defer interment expenses must be paid by the veteran's county of residence.

Montana Employment Benefits

Point Preference in Hiring Veterans
Whenever a public employer uses a scored procedure, an applicant for an initial hiring, must have added to the applicant's score the following percentage points of the total possible points that may be granted in the scored procedure:

- 5 percentage points if the applicant is a veteran; and
- 10 percentage points if the applicant is a disabled veteran or an eligible relative.

A disabled veteran who receives 10 percentage points may not receive an additional 5 percentage points.

Whenever a public employer uses a selection procedure other than a scored procedure, the public employer shall give preference to a disabled veteran, eligible relative, or veteran, in that order, over any non-preferred applicant holding substantially equal qualifications.

Montana Education Benefits

Charges for Tuition -- Waivers
The regents may prescribe tuition rates, matriculation charges, and incidental fees for students in institutions under their jurisdiction.

The regents may:

- waive nonresident tuition for selected and approved nonresident students, not to exceed at any unit 2% of the full-time equivalent enrollment at that unit during the preceding year for:
  - residents of Montana who served with the armed forces of the United States in any of its wars and who were honorably discharged from military service;
  - children of residents of Montana who served with the armed forces of the United States in any of its wars and who were killed in action or died as a result of injury, disease, or other disability incurred while in the service of the armed forces of the United States;
  - the spouses or children of residents of Montana who have been declared to be prisoners of war or missing in action; or
  - the spouse or children of a Montana national guard member who was killed or died as a result of injury, disease, or other disability incurred in the line of duty while serving on state active duty;

Regents may waive tuition for up to 5,000 credits each academic year in accordance with the Montana National Guard education benefit program established by the department of military affairs. The waivers provided are intended to be available for up to 5 years after the person qualifies.

Other Montana State Veteran Benefits

Aid by State, County, and Municipal Officers
All state, county, and municipal officers shall render such aid to the board as shall be within their power and consistent with the duties of their respective offices.

Special Plates for Military Personnel, Veterans, and Spouses
Active military personnel, veterans, or the surviving spouse of an eligible veteran, if the spouse has not remarried, may be issued special military or veteran license plates.

Veterans' Cemetery Fee for Special Veteran License Plates

An applicant for special veteran license plates shall pay $10 for each set issued, renewed, or transferred, in addition to any other taxes or fees applicable. Fees collected under this section must be deposited in the state general fund and transferred to the special revenue account for state veterans' cemeteries.

Vehicle Registration Fee and Veterans' Cemetery Fee Waivers

Eligible persons are exempt from the veterans' cemetery fee for two sets of special veteran license plates and all motor vehicle registration fees for two motor vehicles that are not used for commercial purposes.

Veterans' Clubhouse Exemption -- Incompetent Veterans' Trusts

A clubhouse or building erected by or belonging to any society or organization of honorably discharged United States military personnel that is used primarily for educational, fraternal, benevolent, or purely public charitable purposes rather than for gain or profit, together with the personal property necessarily used in the building, is exempt from taxation. The exemption provided for in this section applies even if a business, intended primarily for the use of the members, is required to be open to the public and is operated in a portion of the building.

All property, real or personal, in the possession of legal guardians of incompetent veterans of U.S. military service or minor dependents of the veterans, when the property is funds or derived from funds received from the United States as pension, compensation, insurance, adjusted compensation, or gratuity, is exempt from all taxation as property of the United States while held by the guardian, but not after title passes to the veteran or minor in the minor's own right on account of removal of legal disability.

Hunting and Fishing Licenses

Persons with disabilities are entitled to fish and to hunt game birds, not including turkeys, with only a conservation license if they are residents of Montana not residing in an institution and are certified as disabled as prescribed by departmental rule. A person who has purchased a conservation license and a resident fishing license or game bird license for a particular license year and who is subsequently certified as disabled is entitled to a refund for the fishing license or game bird license previously purchased for that license year. A person who is certified as disabled pursuant to subsection (3) and who was issued a permit to hunt from a vehicle for license year 2000 or a subsequent license year is automatically entitled to a permit to hunt from a vehicle for subsequent license years if the criteria for obtaining a permit does not change.

State Veterans' Cemeteries

The board shall establish and operate state veterans' cemeteries.

A cemetery must be located at Fort William Henry Harrison in Lewis and Clark County, Montana, and at Miles City. A cemetery may be located in Missoula County and in Yellowstone County if funding allows.

Note: Family of the deceased must apply for County/State benefits BEFORE the deceased is interned.

Nebraska State Veteran's Benefits

The state of Nebraska provides several veteran benefits. This section offers a brief description of each of the following benefits.

- Veterans Homes
- Financial Assistance Benefits
- Education Benefits
- Other State Veteran Benefits

Nebraska Veterans Homes

Veterans who served on active duty in the armed forces of the United States may be eligible for admission to one of the Nebraska veterans homes; eligibility may extend to the spouse, widow(er), and Gold Star parent.

Nebraska Financial Assistance Benefits

Nebraska Veterans' Aid Fund
The NVA Fund was established in 1921. This temporary emergency aid fund assists veterans, their spouses, and dependents when an unforeseen emergency occurs disrupting their normal method of living and when other resources are not immediately available.

For NVA purposes, veteran means any person who
All income from the Fund is used for aid and not for administrative expenses of the fund. Aid can only be used for food, fuel, shelter, wearing apparel, funeral, medical, and surgical items. Application must be made through the County Service Officer or post Service Officer of any recognized veterans' organization in the county nearest the applicant's place of residence and submitted to the Department of Veterans' Affairs

Nebraska Education Benefits

Waiver of Tuition
The University of Nebraska, the state colleges, and community colleges on behalf of any eligible child, spouse, widow or widower that meets the following requirements may waive tuition. He or she is a resident of this state and meets the appropriate institutions requirements for paying in-state tuition. He or she has a parent, stepparent or spouse who was a member of the armed forces of the United States and who: (1) Died of a service connected disability; (2) Died subsequent to discharge as a result of injury or illness sustained while in service; (3) Is permanently and totally disabled as a result of military service; (4) Is classified as missing in action or as a prisoner of war during armed hostilities after August 4,

1964. The waiver shall be valid for one degree, diploma, or certificate from a community college and one baccalaureate degree. Applications are submitted to the Department of Veterans' Affairs by contacting the County Veterans Service Officer nearest the applicant?s place of residence.

Other Nebraska State Veteran Benefits

Game & Parks Commission
Disabled Veterans are eligible for the Veteran Disabled Permits (good for life, no renewal).

Nebraska Veterans' Service Office
The function of the State Service Office is to interview military veterans, their spouses, and dependents to establish tentative eligibility for veterans' benefits provided by federal and state laws; to advise applicants with claims before the US Department of Veterans' Affairs (VA); and to assist them in the accurate completion of application forms and transmit them to the proper federal or state agency for processing. State Service Officers are recognized representatives for the Nebraska Department of Veterans' Affairs, American Legion, Veterans of Foreign Wars, Vietnam Veterans of America, American Ex-POWs, Military Order of the Purple Heart, the Retired Enlisted Association and the National Association of County Service Officers and are authorized to accept Power of Attorneys from claimants on behalf of the organizations. State Service Officers are located at the VA Regional Office, Lincoln.

Discharges
The Department has approximately 700,000 discharges of Nebraska veterans on microfilm. If a veteran entered from and returned to Nebraska upon separation from military service, a copy of the discharge may be on file in the Department. Documents previously filed with the Selective Service System and National Guard were referred to the Department of Veterans' Affairs. Since October 1, 1979, if requested by the service-member, Military Separation Centers have sent a copy of the Certificate of Release or Discharge from active duty (DD214) to the Department.

Grave Registration
The Department of Veterans' Affairs shall preserve a permanent registry of the graves of all persons who shall have served in the Armed Forces of the U.S. in time of war and whose mortal remains rest in Nebraska. Information concerning the registry can be obtained from the Department of Veterans' Affairs or a County Service Officer.

Nevada State Veteran's Benefits

The state of Nevada provides several veteran benefits. This section offers a brief description of each of the following benefits.

- Housing Benefits
- Financial Assistance Benefits
- Employment Benefits

- Other State Veteran Benefits

Nevada Veteran Housing Programs

Nevada Veterans' Home
A State-owned and operated veterans' home is located in Boulder City. The home consists of an extended care facility for veterans in need of skilled nursing home care. Future plans call for a Veterans Home in Northern Nevada.

Nevada Financial Assistance Benefits

Veterans Tax Exemption
An annual tax exemption is available to any veteran with wartime service (including in-theater service during the Persian Gulf War, Afghanistan and Iraqi Wars). To obtain this exemption, take a copy of your DD214 or discharge papers to your local County Assessor.

The exemption can be applied to a veteran's vehicle privilege tax or real property tax. The exemption cannot be split between the two. To obtain the exact amount of this benefit, contact your County Assessor. Veterans may also "donate" their exempted tax directly to the Nevada Veterans' Home Account, which will contribute the amount toward the operation of a Veterans' Home in Nevada.

Disabled Veteran Tax Exemption
Nevada offers a property tax exemption to any veteran with a service-connected disability of 60% or more.

The amounts of exemption that are or will be available to disabled veterans varies from $6,250 to $20,000 of assessed valuation, depending on the percentage of disability and the year filed. To qualify, the veteran must have an honorable separation from the service and be a resident of Nevada.

The widow or widower of a disabled veteran, who was eligible for this exemption at the time of his or her death, may also be eligible to receive this exemption.

This exemption can be applied to a veteran's vehicle tax or personal property tax. To determine the actual value of this benefit or to obtain further information, contact your local county assessor's office.

Nevada Employment Benefits

Civil Service Preference
Civil service preference is given to veterans applying for State employment in Nevada. Veterans with service-connected disabilities receive additional preference.

Other Nevada State Veteran Benefits

Assistance With Claims
Any veteran family member of a veteran, or Nevada resident on Active Duty can receive free

assistance in filing a claim with the U.S. Department of Veterans Affairs for a service-connected disability, pension or other benefit program. Assistance includes help in filing claims, representation at local hearings, appeals and discharge upgrades.

Hunting and Fishing License
The State of Nevada Wildlife Division will issue free hunting fishing licenses to any honorably separated veteran who has a service-connected disability of 50% or more.

Guardianship Program
Nevada State Law permits the Nevada Office of Veterans' Services to act as the financial guardian for incompetent veterans, their widows and children.

Veteran Cemetery Plots
Eligible veterans and members of their immediate family may be buried at the Northern Nevada Veterans Memorial Cemetery in Fernley, or at the Southern Nevada Veterans Memorial Cemetery in Boulder City. There is no charge for the plot, vault and opening & closing of a gravesite for a Veteran. A $350 fee (subject to change) is charged for the burial of the spouse or dependent of a veteran.

Disabled Parking Privileges
The State of Nevada authorizes special parking permits for physically disabled persons. Applications are available at your local DMV office or can be obtained by contacting the DMV Special Plate Section in Carson City.

Special Veteran License Plates
The Nevada Department of Motor Vehicles offers several distinctive license plates for veterans that include:

Ex-Prisoner of War
Disabled Veteran
Purple Heart
Veteran
Pearl Harbor Survivors & Veterans
Congressional Medal of Honor

Applications for special plates can be obtained at your local DMV Office.

Documents
Veterans or their dependents filing claims for service-connected disabilities may receive a one-time free copy of their birth, divorce, death or marriage certificate from the appropriate county courthouse.

Recording Fees
Discharge certificates are recorded free of charge to eligible veterans by Nevada Count Recorders.

New Hampshire State Veteran's Benefits

The state of New Hampshire provides several veteran benefits. This section offers a brief description of each of the following benefits.

- Housing Benefits
- Financial Assistance Benefits
- Employment Benefits
- Education Benefits
- Other State Veteran Benefits

New Hampshire Veteran Housing Programs

Veterans' Home
Located at Tilton, the Veterans' Home is a 250-bed facility for honorably-discharged veterans who have served for a period of at least 90 days in the armed forces of the United States in time of war and who have been New Hampshire residents for one year preceding application. Some restrictions on assets and medical treatment exist.

New Hampshire Financial Assistance Benefits

Bonuses
Bonus of $100 for those with active service of 90 days or more between August 5, 1964, and August 15, 1973, or those who served in Vietnam between July 1, 1958, and August 5, 1964, and earned the Vietnam Service Medal or the Armed Forces Expeditionary Medal. Must have been a bona fide resident of New Hampshire at the time of enlistment and have received an honorable discharge. Claims made afte August 22, 1977, must be approved by the Adjutant General and the Governor and Executive Council.

Persian Gulf War Bonus of $100. Each person who actively served as a member of the armed forces of the United States between August 2, 1990, and November 30, 1995, and who earned the Southwest Asia Service Medal, and who was discharged, released or has a certificate of service therefrom, under honorable conditions, and who at the time of entry on such service, and at the time of such service was a bona fide resident of this state shall be entitled to a $100 bonus. However, no individual who has received a Persian Gulf War Bonus payment from another state shall be qualified to receive the NH bonus. Program expires August 31, 2002, but there are provisions that allow for acceptance of applications after that date.

Global War on Terrorism Operations Service Bonus of $100. Each person who actively served in any capacity as a member of the uniformed services of the United States on or after September 11, 2001 and on or before a date to be determined by the Secretary of Defense, and who earned the Global War on Terrorism Expeditionary Medal or Afghanistan Campaign, or Iraq Campaign Medal; and who was discharged, released or has a certificate of service therefrom, with an honorable discharge, or who is missing in action or who was killed in action; and who at the time of entry on such active service, and at the time of such service was a bona fide resident of this state shall be entitled to the benefits provided under this subdivision. Program ends on June 11, 2009, but there are provisions that allow for acceptance of applications after that date.

Tax Exemption
Property owned and operated by certain veterans' organizations or departments, local chapters or posts shall be exempt from taxation.
Certain wartime veterans, their wives or widows may be eligible for a property tax credit of $50 ($100 if both are eligible veterans). Cities/towns may vote to adopt a higher tax credit of up to $500.

The widow of a veteran who was killed while on active duty in the military may be eligible for a tax credit of between $700 and $2000 on real estate or personal property.

There is a $700 tax credit on real estate occupied as principal place of abode by a permanently and totally disabled service-connected veteran, double amputee or paraplegic or unremarried surviving spouse. Cities and towns may vote to adopt a higher tax credit of up to $2000.

A permanently and totally disabled veteran who is blind, paraplegic or a double amputee as a result of service connection and who owns a specially adapted homestead acquired with the assistance of the U.S. Department of Veterans Affairs, or with proceeds from the sale of any previous homestead acquired with the assistance of the U.S. Department of Veterans Affairs, shall be exempt from all taxation on the homestead. The veteran's surviving spouse shall also be exempt from all taxation on the homestead.

New Hampshire Employment Benefits

Employment Preference
Preference shall be given in appointing employees of the State Liquor Commission, in selecting members of the State Veterans Council, in appointing the Director of the State Veterans Council, in appointing the Commandant and employees of the New Hampshire Veterans Home, and veterans or their unremarried widows and spouses of disabled veterans in public departments and/or public works of state and local units.

Training
Reemployment of veterans by towns and other political subdivisions upon application being made within 90 days after the veteran is discharged from active military service.

New Hampshire Education Benefits

Free Tuition at Vocational-Technical College
The child of a missing person who was domiciled in this State serving in or with the U.S. armed forces after February 28, 1961, is entitled to free tuition at vocational-technical college

so long as said missing person is so reported/listed as missing, captured, etc.

Free Tuition for Surviving Children of Military Members
Children of military members who die in service during wartime, and children of certain wartime veterans who die from a service-connected disability, may qualify for free tuition at New Hampshire public institutions of higher learning. A scholarship for board, room, rent, books and supplies up to $2500 per year for a period of no more than 4 years at such educational institutions may be furnished to these children if they are in need of financial assistance.

Other New Hampshire State Veteran Benefits

Burial
Indigent veterans may be buried at the expense of the municipality in which the veteran died.

Veterans Cemetery
Veterans are eligible for interment in the State Veterans Cemetery in Boscawen, NH. The cemetery opened in September 1997.

Claims
Copies of public records are provided free when needed by the U.S. Department of Veterans Affairs to determine eligibility for benefits. The State Veterans Council and its veterans service officers shall assist veterans and dependents in obtaining benefits to which entitled under state or federal laws or regulations.

License Fee Exemption
Honorably discharged veterans who are residents of New Hampshire and who are permanently and totally disabled from service-connected disability may be issued a free perpetual Fish and Game License.

Patients at the V.A. Medical Center in Manchester, NH, and residents of the NH Veterans' Home may be issued free fishing permits under certain conditions.
Service-connected disabled veterans and their unremarried widows may be exempt from fees for a Peddler's License.

An amputee or paraplegic classified by the U.S. Department of Veterans Affairs as permanently and totally disabled from service-connected disability who owns a motor vehicle received from or replaced by the Department of Veterans Affairs may be furnished a special license plate without charge for one motor vehicle. Recipients of the Purple Heart and Survivors of Pearl Harbor may be issued one set of special license plates upon payment of registration fees.

A veteran determined by the U.S. Department of Veterans Affairs to be totally blind because of a service-connected disability who owns a motor vehicle may be furnished a special license plate without charge for one vehicle.

Special license plates are available without charge to veterans who are former Prisoners of

111

War (POWs).

Special license plates may be issued for motor vehicles owned by individuals with walking disabilities.

No registration fee is payable for a vehicle provided by the U.S. Department of Veterans Affairs to an amputee, paraplegic or blind veteran classified as being permanently and totally disabled from service connection.

Any motor vehicle bearing special disabled veteran license plates shall be allowed free parking time in any city or town if the vehicle is under the direct control of the owner.

No fee shall be charged for a permit to register a motor vehicle owned by a veteran who has been classified by the U.S. Department of Veterans Affairs as being totally blind as a result of a service connected disability.

No fee shall be charged for a permit to register a motor vehicle owned by a war veteran who is an amputee, paraplegic or who suffered the loss of use of a limb from a service connected cause as certified by the U.S. Department of Veterans Affairs when the vehicle is received or a cash settlement in lieu thereof is received from the U.S. Department of Veterans Affairs.

No fee shall be charged for a motor vehicle operator's license for a veteran who is an amputee or paraplegic and who received a motor vehicle from the U.S. Department of Veterans Affairs nor for a veteran who has been classified by the U.S. Department of Veterans Affairs as being permanently and totally disabled due to service connected disability.

Visit the New Hampshire Office of Veterans Services website for contact information and benefits assistance.

Relief
Disabled veterans may hunt from motor vehicles or boats under certain conditions with a proper permit.
War veterans and their dependent families who are unable to support themselves shall be supported at public expense in the town or city in which they live.

State Park Admission
NH veterans with any VA service-connected disability rating shall not be charged a fee for day-use admission to NH state parks. Disabled veteran license plates issued by the state of NH, or a letter issued by the VA certifying the veteran suffers from a service-connected disability shall be considered proof of entitlement. Any fees for the use of enterprise activities (including ski lifts, food service, campgrounds, etc.) shall be charged.
Any active member of a federally-recognized unit of the NH national guard who is a legal resident of this state and is serving (or who retired) in pay grades E-1 through E-6 shall not be charged a fee for admission to the state park system. Any fees for the use of enterprise activities (including ski lifts, food service, campgrounds, etc.) shall be charged.

Veterans License Plate

Veterans honorably discharged from the U.S. Armed Forces may be issued a special license plate. The plate will only be issued upon application, submission of proof of honorable discharge.

New Jersey State Veteran's Benefits

The state of New Jersey provides several veteran benefits. This section offers a brief description of each of the following benefits.

- Housing Benefits
- Financial Assistance Benefits
- Employment Benefits
- Education Benefits
- Other State Veteran Benefits

New Jersey Veteran Housing Programs

NJ Veterans Memorial Homes
If you're responsible for the long-term care and well being of a New Jersey veteran, a New Jersey Veterans Memorial Home may be the right nursing home choice for your loved one.

If you are interested in applying to one of our veterans homes, please contact the homes directly.

Programs include ceramics, dinner parties, socials, bingo, shopping, movies, and games. Off-site events include day trips to places such as Atlantic City, the racetrack, and many sporting events. Other services provided at each home include barber and beauty shops, lounges and recreation rooms, outdoor patios, chapels, snack bars, transportation, and libraries.

Stand Down Operations
Stand Down helps the New Jersey's homeless veterans "combat" life on the streets by providing a broad range of necessities, including food, clothing, medical, legal and mental health assistance, job counseling, and referrals, but most importantly, companionship and camaraderie.

Membership is open to Veterans and volunteers over the age of 18 who are willing and able to give of their time, efforts and resources in assisting programs for homeless veterans..

Veterans Haven
The Transitional Housing Program for homeless veterans occupies one large building on state property in Winslow Township. The program is divided into three phases: treatment; self-reclamation; and community reintegration. Each phase lasts three to six months and is tailored to individual treatment needs and vocational interests.

Eligible veterans are referred from a VA Medical Center after receiving a medical evaluation. To be admitted into the program, the veteran must agree to a long-term program focusing on psychological, social and vocational rehabilitation. The program is drug and alcohol free, and has a staff comprised of professionals in the fields of mental health, addictions, social work, vocational rehabilitation and nursing.

NJ Housing and Mortgage Finance Agency (HMFA)
The New Jersey Housing and Mortgage Finance Agency (HMFA) offers low interest rate HMFA mortgages that provide veterans and their families with increased buying power and a savings of thousands of dollars in interest over the life of the loan. HMFA offers residential mortgages to United States veterans through the Veterans Administration (VA) home buyer program. Most HMFA homeownership loans are originated by private lenders that are approved to participate in the programs.

New Jersey Financial Assistance Benefits

New Jersey State Income Tax Exclusions

U.S. military pension and survivor's benefit payments are not taxable for New Jersey gross income tax purposes, regardless of the recipient's age or disability status. The exemption of military pensions from New Jersey gross income tax began in tax year 2001.

New Jersey Property Tax Deduction
There is an annual property tax deduction of two hundred and fifty dollars for eligible veterans.

Filing an application with all required documentation prior to December 31 of the pre-tax year in order to be effective in the next year. Documentation includes the property deed and discharge (DD-214) for the veteran. The widow may need to submit the property deed, marriage certificate, death certificate and discharge (DD-214).

New Jersey Property Tax Exemption
Eligibility for Veterans who meet all of the following criteria:

- Served during a specified wartime period.

- Received an honorable discharge or under honorable conditions.

- Rated 100 percent permanent service-connected by the VA. The 100 percent rating cannot be temporary or as a result of hospitalization, surgery or recuperation.

The exemption unlike the deduction is PRORATED from the date the veteran or spouse filed the application with ALL required documentation. EXAMPLE: A veteran completes the application on April 7, but does not submit all the documentation until May 3. The veteran's property tax exemption is effective May 3. Many tax assessors exempt the property tax January 1 of the next year. The same proration process applies to the surviving spouse.

New Jersey Employment Benefits

Veterans Preference and Pension Status
NJ Department of Military and Veterans Affairs is the agency to determine veterans preference for hiring in New Jersey civil service and veterans status for New Jersey civil service pension plans.

Veterans Preference for Hiring in New Jersey Civil Service
The NJ Department of Military and Veterans Affairs is the agency that determines veterans preference for hiring in New Jersey civil service and veteran status for New Jersey civil

service pension plans.

Veterans Preference for Hiring in New Jersey Civil Service: War period veterans who pass state civil service examinations are given absolute preference over non-veterans when applying for state, county and municipal employment. Absolute preference is not extended to promotions, but if a veteran ranks highest on a promotional certification, a non-veteran cannot be offered the appointment before the veteran. Veterans with service-connected disabilities (at least 10%) who pass civil service examinations are given preference over other veterans and non-veterans for state, county and municipal employment.

Veterans Status for Civil Service and Pension Plans
A pension is available to qualified veterans. To qualify, a veteran must apply for veterans status for civil service pension plans after employment and must be in active employment until the effective date of retirement. These benefits cannot be deferred. Veterans who continue in employment covered by Public Employees' Retirement System (PERS) until they are at least age 60 with 20 or more years of service credit are entitled to an annual benefit equal to one-half of the salary on which pension contributions were made in any consecutive 12-month period which would provide the largest possible benefit to the member.

Veterans who are at least age 55 with 35 or more years of service credit are entitled to an annual allowance based on the following formula: Years of Service divided by 55, multiplied by the last 12 months salary, which yields the Maximum Annual Allowance. Veterans benefits cannot be deferred and members must meet all the requirements to qualify. Veteran members may retire on the same basis as non-veteran members if it would result in a higher benefit.

Other Civil Service Benefits for Veterans Preference
The following are other civil service benefits for veterans preference:

- Appointment of veterans
- Application of statutes to promotions
- Preference in appointment in noncompetitive division
- Preference to veterans in layoffs
- Hearing on dismissal of veterans
- Veterans not to be discriminated against because of physical defects

Employment or Promotion
Any individual who has served in the Army, Air Force, Navy, or Marine Corps of the United States and who has been awarded the Medal of Honor, the Distinguished Service Cross, Air Force Cross or Navy Cross, while a resident of this State, and any individual who has served in the United States Coast Guard and who has been awarded the Medal of Honor or the Navy Cross while a resident of this State, shall be appointed or promoted without complying with the rules of the Merit System Board. The appointing authority to whom the individual applies for appointment or promotion shall, at its discretion, appoint or promote that person. Upon promotion or appointment, that person shall become subject to the rules of the Merit System Board. A person who qualifies under this section shall not be limited to only one appointment or promotion.

New Jersey Education Benefits

Operation Recognition: High School Diplomas for Veterans
The New Jersey Department of Military and Veterans Affairs (DMAVA) and the Department of Education jointly launched a program October 5, 2000 to honor World War II era veterans who left school to join the military and never received a high school diploma. Known as Operation Recognition, the program will award a state-endorsed high school diploma to any New Jersey veteran who left a New Jersey high school to enter military service during World War II. Because of the overwhelming success of this program, The Adjutant General and the Commissioner of Education are expanding the program to include veterans from the Korean and Vietnam wars.

State Approving Agency
This office approves and supervises programs for the G.I. Bill for use in colleges, non-college degree programs, apprenticeship, on-the-job training, flight, and correspondence schools.

POW and MIA Tuition Benefits
Free undergraduate college tuition is available to any child born or adopted before, during or after the period of time his or her parent was officially declared a prisoner of war (POW) or person missing in action (MIA) after Jan. 1, 1960. The POW-MIA must have been a New Jersey resident at the time he or she entered the service or whose official residence is in New Jersey. The child must attend either a public or private institution in New Jersey. A copy of DD- 1300 must be furnished with the application.

War Orphans Tuition Assistance
Children of those service personnel who died while in the military or due to service-connected disabilities, or who are officially listed as missing in action by the U.S. Dept. of Defense may claim $500 per year for four years of college or equivalent training. To qualify, the child must be a resident of New Jersey for at least one year immediately preceding the filing of the application and be between the ages of 16 and 21 at the time of application. The veteran must have been a state resident.

Vietnam Veterans Tuition Credit Program
The Vietnam Veterans Tuition Credit Program provides additional education benefits to veterans eligible for federally funded education programs and who served on active duty from December 31, 1960 to May 7, 1975 and who were legal residents of New Jersey at the time of induction into the Armed Forces or at the time of discharge from active service or for a period not less than one year prior to making application. The amount of the award is $400 annually or $200 per semester for full-time attendance and $100 per semester for part-time. Deadlines for applying are October 1 and March 1.

New Jersey National Guard Educational Benefits
New Jersey National Guardsman (Army or Air) who are eligible must:

- Have completed Initial Active Duty Training.
- Be in good standing with your unit.

Tuition Assistance: Pays up to 75% of tuition costs at Accredited schools only with a maximum of $100 per undergraduate credit and a maximum of $170 per graduate credit. Tuition Assistance may NOT be used together with any other federal program (i.e. the GI Bill)

Other New Jersey State Veteran Benefits

Replacement of Medals
Veterans may request issuance or replacement of their medals and awards. Family members may only request medals and awards of living veterans by obtaining their signed authorizations. For deceased veterans, requests will be accepted from next-of-kin (unremarried widow or widower, son or daughter, father or mother, brother or sister of the deceased veteran.)

Fishing and Hunting Licenses
The NJ Division of Fish & Wildlife will annually issue the following items FREE to each qualified disabled veteran: a fire arm, bow & arrow, fishing or all around hunting license, a pheasant and quail stamp, a state duck stamp and a trout stamp. In addition, disabled veterans may apply for free permits: one bow and arrow deer permit *; one firearm (muzzleloader or shotgun) deer permit *; one spring and one fall turkey permit * for use during applicable hunting season.

*Special deer and turkey permit applications will be available at the Division offices listed below or by mail from the Trenton office. All rules and regulations pertaining to the lottery system and laws for each season still apply. In other words, you will be allowed to enter the first lottery and fall lottery for free but will not be guaranteed a permit. Your odds of winning a permit depend upon what zone and/or time period you select. Additional permits for added hunting opportunities may be purchased at the current rate of $28.00.

No Fee Automobile Registration
The veteran must be 100 percent disabled and:

- also be eligible for the automobile financial assistance from the U.S. Department of Veterans Affairs (VA).

In addition, the veteran must have sustained the following injuries incurred or aggravated during active military service:

- loss or permanent loss of use of one or both feet

- loss or permanent loss of use of one or both hands

- permanent impairment of vision of both eyes to a prescribed degree. Veterans with best-corrected vision no better than 20/200 or less or field defect of 20 degrees or less are considered eligible.

No Fee Automobile Registration for Medal of Honor Recipients: Medal of Honor recipients are eligible for a no-fee registration and will receive special license plates noting their award. Contact - For information call 1-888-486-3339.

State Parks Admission
The New Jersey Division of State Parks and Forestry does not charge an admission fee for entrance into a State park or forest by any resident of the State who is an active member of the New Jersey National Guard who has completed Initial Active Duty Training.

Brigadier General William C. Doyle Veterans Memorial Cemetery
Free interment and perpetual care, in the Brigadier General William C. Doyle Veterans Memorial Cemetery, is available to veteran residents of New Jersey, their spouses and

dependant children. The Brigadier General William C. Doyle Veterans Memorial Cemetery is located at 350 Provinceline Road, Wrightstown, NJ 08562.

The BG William C. Doyle Veterans Memorial Cemetery, a state- operated cemetery dedicated to veterans, is located on 225 acres in a picturesque setting of partially wooded land in Arneytown, North Hanover Township, Burlington County. The cemetery features a modern, nondenominational chapel/administration building. The cemetery will accommodate 215,000 veterans and eligible family members. Areas are provided for the interment of those cremated and for those veterans whose remains have never been recovered.

New Mexico State Veteran's Benefits

The state of New Mexico provides several veteran benefits. This section offers a brief description of each of the following benefits.

- Housing Benefits
- Financial Assistance Benefits
- Education Benefits
- Other State Veteran Benefits

New Mexico Veteran Housing Programs

Homeless and At Risk Veteran Services
Through the New Mexico Veterans Integration Center (NMVIC) in Albuquerque, DVS provides transition services for homeless and at risk NM veterans.

The NMVIC facility at 13032 Central Ave SE provides housing, meal service and a continuum of support services designed to assist homeless veterans to self-sufficiency.

Contact them at:
Office (505)265-0512
Residential: (505)275-8200 Ext.118
Email: info@nmvic.org

New Mexico Financial Assistance Benefits

Veterans' Tax Exemption
Any veteran who was honorably discharged from the U.S. Armed Forces and served 90 or more days of active duty and has established legal residency in New Mexico, qualifies for the New Mexico Veterans' Tax Exemption.

Disabled Veteran Tax Exemption
Any veteran who has been approved for 100 percent service-connected disability compensation benefits by the Department of Veterans Affairs (VA) is eligible for a complete property tax waiver on their primary residence.

New Mexico Education Benefits

In-State Tuition for Veterans and Dependents of Active Duty (including Title 10 Reserve and Guard) Members

All honorably discharged veterans using a federal education benefit and dependents of Active Duty, Guard and Reserve (title 10) Servicemembers--regardless of where they live--qualify as residents and therefore pay reduced 'resident' or in-state tuition rates and fees at all state operated institutions of higher learning in New Mexico. This eliminates the waiting period needed to qualify as a resident of the state.

Call the NMDVS office at (866) 433-8387 for more details.

Vietnam Veteran Scholarship
Veterans who have been residents of New Mexico for a minimum of 10 years, served in Vietnam, and were issued the Vietnam Campaign or Service Medal are eligible. The Vietnam Veteran Scholarship will pay full tuition and books at any state funded post-secondary school.

World War II and Korean Veterans High School Diploma
Any WWII or Korean War veteran who joined the Armed Forces while attending a New Mexico high school prior to graduation is eligible for a high school diploma.

Veterans Education and Training Services
The State Approval Office is responsible for evaluating and approving education and job training programs under U.S. Department of Veterans Affairs, GI Bill regulations.

Other New Mexico State Veteran Benefits

Children of Deceased Veterans
Children between the ages of 16-26 whose veteran parent was killed in action or died as a result of their wounds incurred in battle, qualify for a full tuition waiver at any state funded post-secondary school. A $150 stipend, per semester, will be issued to help with books or fees.

Disabled Veterans Hunting and Fishing License
Any veteran rated 100 percent service-connected disabled, qualifies for a free lifetime small game hunting and fishing license in the State of New Mexico.

Veterans' License Plates
Any veteran who was honorably discharged from the Armed Forces of the U.S. is eligible for a New Mexico license plate. A fee and registration is required for some plates.

- Armed Forces Plate
- Purple Heart
- 100% Disabled Veteran
- Pearl Harbor Survivor
- Purple Heart
- Ex-POW

- Medal of Honor

The Patriot Plate
Enabled by 2006 legislation, the Patriot Plate is a special license plate that provides the public with an opportunity to recognize the contributions and sacrifices of the men and women of the U.S. Armed Forces.

Veterans' Military Honors
Coordinates with military and local veteran organizations to provide an honor guard and bugler for military honors funerals for deceased veterans.

Veteran Transportation Service
Provides statewide transportation for veterans to the Department of Veterans Affairs Medical Center and its satellite clinics for scheduled appointments. DVS contracts with DAV.

Native American Outreach Services
Coordinates outreach and training programs for tribal members statewide to provide information and assistance for Native veterans.

New York State Veteran's Benefits

The state of New York provides several veteran benefits. This section offers a brief description of each of the following benefits.

- Housing Benefits
- Financial Assistance Benefits
- Employment Benefits
- Education Benefits
- Other State Veteran Benefits

New York Veteran Housing Programs

State Veterans Home
A 242 bed veterans home is operated by the State Department of Health at Oxford, Chenango County, for veterans, spouses and certain parents. The Department of Health also operates a 250-bed facility at St. Albans, Queens, a 126-bed facility adjacent to the Veterans Affairs Medical Center in Batavia, Genesee County and a 250-bed facility in Montrose, Westchester County.

A 350-bed Veterans Home is located on the campus of the State University of New York at Stony Brook, Long Island, and is operated by the university's Health Sciences Center. Health related care and skilled nursing services are available at all facilities. Admission preference is based on severity of illness or disability and need for care.

New York State Homes For Veterans Program

Homes for Veterans Program offers fixed-rate mortgages with interest rates 0.5% below the already low interest rates charged on SONYMA mortgages with closing cost assistance.

New York Financial Assistance Benefits

Property Tax Exemption
Partial exemption from real property taxes is based on condition of service, with additional benefits based upon degree of service-connected disability. Applications must be filed before Taxable Status Day. Qualifying widow(er)s may file for benefit based on their spouse's service. Exemption applies to local and county property taxes.

Supplemental Burial Allowance
A supplemental burial allowance of up to $6,000 is authorized for certain military personnel killed in combat or while on active duty in hostile or imminent danger locations on or after September 29, 2003.

New York State Blind Annuity
A New York State Blind Annuity (2008 rate is $1,128.72 annually) is available to visually impaired wartime veterans and certain unremarried spouses. For More Information, Call 1-888-838-7697 or 518-486-3602

New York State Gold Star Annuity
Gold Star Parent Annuity authorizes an annuity payment of up to $500 per Gold Star parent of a deceased veteran.

New York Employment Benefits

Disabled Veterans Civil Service Preference
Qualified handicapped disabled veterans eligible for appointment to non-competitive State employment positions under Sections 55-b and 55-c of the New York State Civil Service Law.

Civil Service Credit Preference
Ten-point additional credit preference toward original appointment for disabled wartime veterans; five-points for wartime service; and two and a half points for competitive promotional exams. Job retention rights applicable to veterans and spouses of totally disabled veterans.

Visit the New York Division of Veterans Services website for contact information and benefits assistance.

New York Education Benefits

Veterans Tuition Awards

Veterans Tuition Awards (VTA) are awards for full-time study and part-time study for eligible veterans matriculated at an undergraduate or graduate degree-granting institution or in an approved vocational training program in New York State.

NOTE: Students previously approved for this award must apply for payment each year. Those students attending a vocational school or who are attending an approved undergraduate or graduate program part-time may apply for payment for the current academic year by completing the supplement.

Award Amounts

- For full-time study, a recipient shall receive an award of up to the full cost of undergraduate tuition for New York state residents at the State University of New York, or actual tuition charged, whichever is less. Full-time study is defined as twelve or more credits per semester (or the equivalent) at a degree-granting institution, or twenty-four or more hours per week in a vocational training program.

- For part-time study, awards will be prorated by credit hour. Part-time study is defined as at least three but fewer than twelve credits per semester (or the equivalent) at a degree-granting institution, or six to twenty-three hours per week in a vocational training program.

Duration:
Full-time Study

- Undergraduate Degree-Granting Programs - Awards are available for up to eight semesters (four years) of undergraduate study. Awards can be made available for up to semesters of undergraduate study for enrollment in an approved five-year program or for enrollment in an approved program of remedial study.

- Graduate Degree-Granting Programs - Awards are available for up to six semesters (three years) of graduate study.

- Vocational Training Programs - Awards are available for up to a maximum of four semesters (two years) of study in an approved vocational training program.

Part-time Study

- Undergraduate Degree-Granting Programs - Awards are available for up to the equivalent of eight semesters (four years) of full-time undergraduate study in a four-year program. Awards can be made available for up to the equivalent of ten semesters (five years) of full-time study for enrollment in an approved five-year undergraduate program which normally requires five academic years of full-time study.

- Graduate Degree-Granting Programs - Awards are available for up to the equivalent of six semesters (three years) of part-time graduate study.

- Vocational Training Programs - Awards are available for up to a maximum of eight semesters (four years) of part-time study in an approved vocational training program.

Approved programs are defined as undergraduate degree, graduate degree, diploma, and certificate programs at degree-granting institutions, or noncredit vocational training programs of at least 320 clock hours specifically approved by the New York State Division of Veteran's Affairs' Bureau of Veterans Education.

Eligible Veterans
Eligible students are those who are New York State residents discharged under honorable conditions from the U.S. Armed forces and who are:

- Vietnam Veterans who served in Indochina between February 28, 1961 and May 7, 1975.

- Persian Gulf Veterans who served in the Persian Gulf on or after August 2, 1990.
- Afghanistan Veterans who served in Afghanistan during hostilities on or after September 11, 2001.
- Veterans of the armed forces of the United States who served in hostilities that occurred after February 28, 1961 as evidenced by receipt of an Armed Forces Expeditionary Medal, Navy Expeditionary Medal or a Marine Corps Expeditionary Medal.

These students must also:

- Establish eligibility by applying to HESC.
- Be New York State residents.
- Be US Citizens or eligible noncitizens.
- Be matriculated full or part- time at an undergraduate or graduate degree-granting institution in New York State or in an approved vocational training program in New York State.
- Have applied for the Tuition Assistance Program for full-time undergraduate or graduate study.

How to Establish Eligibility
Complete the New York State Veterans Tuition Award Supplement or contact HESC. Be sure to print the Web Supplement Confirmation, sign and return it along with the required documentation according to the instructions.

Questions regarding eligible service or how to document service should be directed to the HESC Scholarship Unit at 1-888-697-4372.

How to Apply for Payment
Once you have established your eligibility, you must apply for payment. While you need only establish your eligibility once, you must apply for payment each year.

Apply for payment as follows:

- Undergraduate and Graduate Full-time Study - Apply for payment by doing one of the following:

1. Apply online by completing the Free Application for Federal Student Aid (FAFSA) -- the form used by virtually all colleges, universities and vocational schools for awarding federal student aid and most state and college aid -- and then linking to the TAP on the Web application, or
2. For veterans who do not anticipate filing a FAFSA, complete a Scholarship Grant Payment Application. For a copy of the application call HESC at 1-888-697-4372.

- Undergraduate Part-time Study - Complete only the Veterans Tuition Award Supplement.
- Graduate Part-time Study - Complete only the Veterans Tuition Award Supplement.
- Vocational Training Program - Complete only the Veterans Tuition Award Supplement.

Visit the New York Division of Veterans Services website for contact information and application assistance.

New York State Regents Awards (for Children)
Regents Awards for Children of Deceased & Disabled Veterans provide up to $450 per year to students whose parent(s) served in the US Armed Forces during specified times of national emergency.

Military Service Recognition Scholarship
Available to certain dependents of military personnel killed, severely and permanently disabled or missing in combat or a combat zone of operation since August 2, 1990.

Operation Recognition - High School Diplomas
Operation Recognition allows certain veterans to earn high school diplomas if they left school without graduating.

Other New York State Veteran Benefits

Hunting Licenses & Permits
Veterans with a 40-percent or greater disability rating are eligible for low-cost hunting and fishing licenses, and free use of state parks, historic sites and recreation sites.

Customized Military and Veteran License Plates
Specialty plates for veterans and military members. All vehicles that are registered in NYS as a passenger class vehicle or as a commercial class vehicle are eligible. Certain custom plates are available for Motorcycles also.

North Carolina State Veteran's Benefits

The state of North Carolina provides several veteran benefits. This section offers a brief description of each of the following benefits.

- Housing Benefits
- Financial Assistance Benefits
- Employment Benefits
- Education Benefits
- Other State Veteran Benefits

North Carolina Veteran Housing Programs

North Carolina State Veterans Nursing Homes
The State of North Carolina is proud to offer two full-service, skilled nursing facilities for veterans. One is located adjacent to the VA Medical Center in Fayetteville, NC and the second on the W.G. Hefner Medical Center campus in Salisbury, NC.

Their primary mission is to provide high quality nursing care to veterans, which will improve their quality of life. At the North Carolina State Veterans Nursing Homes, we know how to meet the special needs of veterans. Dedicated to excellence, our highly skilled professional staff provides exceptional care and activities to enrich individuals.

North Carolina Financial Assistance Benefits

Income Tax Relief
Cancellation of Certain Assessments and Abatement of Income Tax: Any assessment of income tax due prior to the time a person was inducted into the Armed Forces will be canceled and abated if the serviceperson was killed while a member of the Armed Forces or is receiving service-connected disability compensation. No interest is payable on refunds made under this section of the law.

Allowances, Servicepersons: Subsistence and quarters allowances, uniform and equipment allowances and mustering-out payments are not taxable to the serviceperson as income. Mileage and per diem allowances for official travel and transportation are excludable from the service income except to the extent that they exceed the travel and transportation expenses.

Deductions, Servicepersons: Income tax deduction may be claimed for insignia, swords, aiguillettes, epaulets, campaign bars, cap devices, chin straps and the cost of altering uniforms necessitated by change in rank.

Disability Pay, U. S. Government: All disability payments to veterans by reason of service in the Armed Forces are not reportable as income for income taxation purposes.

Education and Training Allowances: U. S. Department of Veterans Affairs payments made to veterans enrolled in schools and training establishments under the GI Bill are exempt from income taxation.

Grants for Motor Vehicles: Grants by the U. S. Department of Veterans Affairs for motor vehicles for veterans who lost their sight or the use of their limbs are exempt from income taxation.

Grants for Specially Adapted Housing: Grants by the U. S. Department of Veterans Affairs to seriously disabled veterans for homes designed for wheelchair living are exempt from income taxation.

Gratuity Pay, Six-Months: The six-months gratuity pay to a beneficiary of a deceased serviceperson is exempt from income taxation.

Hostile Fire Duty Pay: Exemption is same as Federal Internal Revenue Service.

Insurance Dividends, Government Insurance: Dividends and all other proceeds except interest on dividends from G. I. insurance policies are exempt from income taxation.

Retired Pay: The following is exempt from income taxation: Any amount, not to exceed $4,000 received by a taxpayer during any year as retired or retainer pay as a result of service in any of the Armed Forces of the United States.

Property Tax Relief
Certain Vehicles. A motor vehicle owned by a disabled veteran that is altered with special equipment to accommodate a service-connected disability. As used in this section, disabled veteran means a person as defined in 38 U.S.C. -- 101(2) who is entitled to special automotive equipment for a service-connected disability.

Specially Adapted Housing. Disabled veterans who receive U. S. Government assistance under Title 38, United States Code Annotated for the acquisition of specially adapted housing are eligible for an exclusion from ad valorem taxation on the first $38,000 in assessed value of housing together with the necessary land therefore which is owned and used as a residence by the disabled veteran.

Veterans Organizations. Real and personal property belonging to veterans organizations as defined by statute shall not be listed, appraised, assessed, or taxed for ad valorem purposes..

North Carolina Employment Benefits

Employment Preference
Preference in State Government employment is granted to veterans, their surviving spouses or the spouses of disabled veterans, without regard to age, provided they are otherwise qualified. Military leave with reemployment rights is also granted State employees. The Employment Service Division of the Employment Security Commission assists in endeavoring to secure suitable employment for disabled veterans. Any person desiring information and assistance with matters related to employment and job placement should contact the nearest local employment office of the Employment Security Commission. Veterans Employment Representatives are available to render specialized service for veterans.

Licensing Law Helps Veterans and Spouse
The North Carolina Governor has signed a new law which permits military-trained applicants who have been awarded a military occupational specialty and military-spouse applicants who are licensed in another jurisdiction to receive occupational licenses in North Carolina. Regardless of occupational specialty, all military or out-of-state qualifications must meet or exceed North Carolina's licensure standards. A licensing board will determine eligibility to qualify for licensing and certification based on training, experience and competency requirements. There are more than a 100 different occupational licensing agencies in North Carolina, and each licensing board will be required to implement the new statute within one year from the date the act becomes law.

North Carolina Education Benefits

Scholarships
Any member of the armed services qualifying for admission to an institution of higher education, but not qualifying as a resident for tuition purposes shall be charged the in-state tuition rate for enrollments while a member of armed services in the state.

Other North Carolina State Veteran Benefits

Guardians
State law provides for the appointment and supervision of guardians for incompetent veterans, incompetent dependents of veterans and minor dependents of members of the armed forces or veterans in certain circumstances, to manage U.S. funds payable to such persons.

Hunting and Fishing Licenses
All 50% or more disabled veterans may obtain a lifetime hunting-fishing license upon the payment of $10.00. Members of the U.S. Armed Forces stationed in North Carolina, their

spouses and their dependents under age 18 residing with them are deemed residents of North Carolina for the purpose of purchasing licenses issued by the Wildlife Resources Commission.

Auto License Plates
The following auto license plates are available to eligible persons:

- American Legion
- Bronze Star Recipient
- Combat Veterans
- Disabled Veteran
- Distinguished Flying Cross
- Legion of Valor
- Military Reservist
- Military Retiree
- National Guard Member
- Partially Disable Veteran
- Pearl Harbor Survivor
- Prisoner of War
- Purple Heart Recipient
- Silver Star Recipient
- Veterans of Foreign Wars
- Vietnam Veteran
- Fees

Drivers License
In general, State law allows a military drivers license expiration procedure within the Division of Motor Vehicles to renew upon request to North Carolina residents on active duty, to their spouses and dependent children.

Handicapped Parking Privileges
Disabled veterans issued a registration plate are entitled to park in spaces designated for the handicapped and unlimited parking time in most parking zones having time restrictions.

Absentee Registration and Voting
Persons who are in the armed forces, their spouses, veterans in government hospitals, etc., who are otherwise qualified to vote may register and vote by mail in primaries and general elections, subject to the procedural details set forth in the law.

Disabled Voters, Primary or General Elections
Assistance in Voting. A voter who, on account of physical disability, blindness or illiteracy is entitled to assistance as prescribed in the law, in getting to and from the voting booth and in marking their ballots.

Voting Outside the Voting Enclosure. Voters who are able to travel to the voting place, but because of age, physical disability or physical barriers encountered at the voting place are unable to enter same without physical assistance, may vote from their vehicles or in the immediate proximity of the voting place, subject to certain procedures prescribed by law.

Records
Discharges. The Register of Deeds of any North Carolina county is required to record, free of charge, all official discharges from the armed forces offered for registration. Free certified copies of discharges so recorded may be obtained by members or former members of the armed forces and by representatives of the N. C. Division of Veterans Affairs upon application.

Other Records, Including Discharges. Representatives of North Carolina Division of Veterans Affairs who need copies of State and local public records in assisting clients may obtain same without charge. Exception: certain privileged and confidential records whose disclosure is otherwise provided for by law.

Certified Copy of Public Record. A certified copy of any public record required by the U. S. Department of Veterans Affairs or the Division of Veterans Affairs for use in determining the eligibility of any person to participate in benefits made available by the U. S. Department of Veterans Affairs shall be provided without charge by the official responsible for the custody of the public record. The document shall be issued to the applicant for such benefits or any person acting on his or her behalf or the representative of the U. S. Department of Veterans Affairs or the Division of Veterans Affairs.

Retirement Credit, Military Service, State and Participating Local Government Employees Under certain conditions and subject to the confines of State law, credit for both State and local government retirement plans can be granted for military service performed by an eligible employee. Further inquiry should be made to Employee's Retirement and Health Benefits Division, N. C. Department of the Treasurer, Raleigh, N. C.

North Dakota State Veteran's Benefits

The state of North Dakota provides several veteran benefits. This section offers a brief description of each of the following benefits.

- Housing Benefits
- Financial Assistance Benefits
- Education Benefits
- Other State Veteran Benefits

North Dakota Veteran Housing Programs

Veterans Home
The North Dakota Veterans Home, located in Lisbon, North Dakota, consists of 111 basic care and 38 skilled nursing beds. The Veterans Home was established to provide service to an eligible veteran who is:

A bona fide resident of North Dakota for at least one year; or
Served in a North Dakota regiment (activated N. D. National Guard); or
Entered the Armed Forces as a North Dakota resident; or
Is the spouse or surviving spouse of above veteran.

Application may be made through any County Veterans Service Officer.

North Dakota Financial Assistance Benefits

Hardship Grant
The purpose of this assistance is to provide monies to give aid and comfort to veterans and their spouses, or unremarried widow/widowers of eligible veterans.

The individual must have an emergency need of dental work, eye glasses, hearing aids, transportation for medical treatment, or any special need approved by the Commissioner of Veterans Affairs.

Loan Program
The Veterans Aid Fund is a permanent fund to be used solely for the purpose of making loans to veterans or their widow/widowers.

To qualify, the applicant is required to be a: peacetime veteran, wartime veteran or, National Guard with active duty, or unremarried widow/widower of eligible veteran; a citizen and resident of North Dakota for at least one year, and have the financial ability to make payments.

The maximum loan amount is $5,000. The interest rate is 8% per annum. Time limit can be from six months to 48 months.

North Dakota Education Benefits

Tuition Waiver
Any qualifying member of the national guard who enrolls in any state-controlled school, shall, subject to national guard rules promulgated by the adjutant general, receive a waiver of the tuition charged by the school.

The tuition waiver is valid only so long as the member of the national guard maintains satisfactory performance with the guard, meets the qualification requirements of rules promulgated by the adjutant general, and pursues a course of study in a manner which satisfies the normal requirements of the school.

Free Tuition to qualified Dependents in North Dakota Institution of Higher Education.

Any dependent of a resident veteran who was killed in action or died from wounds or other service-connected causes, was totally disabled as a result of service-connected causes, died from service-connected disabilities, was a prisoner of war, or was declared missing in action, upon being duly accepted for enrollment into any North Dakota state-supported institution of higher education or state-supported technical or vocational school, must be allowed to obtain a bachelor's degree or certificate of completion, for so long as the dependent is eligible, free of any tuition and fee charges.... provided that the bachelor's degree or certificate of completion is earned within a forty-five month or ten semester period or its equivalent; and further that tuition and fee charges shall not include costs for aviation flight charges or expenses.

Other North Dakota State Veteran Benefits

License Plates
A veteran, while serving in the U.S. armed forces was a prisoner of war and has received an honorable discharge from the U.S. armed forces, may be issued a special number license plate. On the death of the veteran, the surviving spouse may retain the numbered plate as an active plate.

N.D. Veterans' Cemetery
Distinctive numbered plates may be issued to individuals eligible for interment in the North Dakota Veterans' Cemetery. The surcharge collected will be divided between the Veterans' Cemetery Trust Fund and the Veterans' Cemetery Maintenance Fund.

National Guard
Distinctive numbered plates may be issued to members of the National Guard. The Adjutant General shall certify those members of the national guard eligible to receive the plates.

Purple Heart
Available to those recipients of the Purple Heart award as listed on the DD214 or Certificate.

Learn more about License Plates

Transportation
The veterans transportation system is designed to aid veterans in transportation to a Veterans Hospital. Currently, there are 5 vans on scheduled routes bringing veterans to Fargo, North Dakota or Miles City, Montana. The cost of this program is underwritten in part by the Post War Trust Fund.

Ohio State Veteran's Benefits

The state of Ohio provides several veteran benefits. This section offers a brief description of each of the following benefits.

- Housing Benefits
- Financial Assistance Benefits
- Education Benefits
- Other State Veteran Benefits

Ohio Veteran Housing Programs

Ohio Veterans Home
The Ohio Veterans Home Agency is a State of Ohio establishment comprised of two facilities, a home located in Sandusky, Ohio (approximately 60 miles west of Cleveland) and a home located in Georgetown, Ohio (approximately 45 miles east of Cincinnati).

The Georgetown Home is a licensed nursing home providing two levels of nursing care -- standard care and special care (Alzheimer/ Dementia). The Sandusky Home, in addition to offering standard care and special care in its licensed nursing home, also offers Veterans Hall (DOM), a domiciliary for those who are able to function in an independent living situation, and DOM+ for those requiring very limited assistance (supervised care) but who do not require the level of care provided to nursing home residents.

Ohio Financial Assistance Benefits

Ohio Veterans Bonus Program
Eligible Veterans may receive $100 for each month spent on active duty service in the following locations during these specified dates:

- Persian Gulf between August 2, 1990 and March 3, 1991, the date when Iraq accepted the conditions for a permanent cease fire. Eligible Veterans can apply for a bonus until December 31, 2013.

- Afghanistan since October 7, 2001. Eligible Veterans can apply for a bonus for up to three years after the President declares an end to U.S. involvement in Afghanistan.

Iraq since March 19, 2003. Eligible Veterans can apply for a bonus for up to three years after the President declares an end to U.S. involvement in Iraq.

The maximum benefit for in-theater service is $1,000.

Eligible Veterans are encouraged to begin the process by completing the online bonus application. Applications are available at www.veteransbonus.ohio.gov, or at any of Ohio's 88 County Veterans Services Offices. Or call 1 - 877 - OHIO VET to get a paper application. In most cases, applying on-line is the simplest and fastest option. However, the application is not complete until they print, sign and mail the application along with required supporting documentation through the U.S. Postal Service. The signed application must be "notarized" or "acknowledged" and mailed to:

Ohio Veterans Bonus
P.O. Box 373
Sandusky, OH 44871

Compensation and VA Claims
County Veterans Service Officers are extensively trained to assist with the preparation and submission of VA claims, compensation and appeals.

Financial Assistance
Financial assistance is available through your County Veterans Service Office on a short term basis to eligible veterans and their dependents.

Military Injury Relief Fund
Ohio grants money to individuals injured while in active service as a member of the armed forces of the United States and while serving under operation Iraqi freedom or operation enduring freedom. Effective August 21, 2008 MIRF is exempt from State Taxation.

131

Ohio Education Benefits

Ohio War Orphans Scholarship
In order to be eligible for consideration of a scholarship, the child of an eligible person must meet the following requirements: (1) At the time of application, have attained his or her sixteenth but not his or her twenty-first birthday; (2) At the time of application, if a child of a veteran who entered the armed services: (a) As a legal resident of Ohio, have resided in the state for the last preceding year; (b) Not as a legal resident of Ohio, have resided in the state for the year preceding the year in which application for the scholarship is made and any other four of the last ten years; (3) Be in financial need, as determined by the Board.

Ohio GI Promise
In an effort to enhance the benefits for veterans established in the federal Post-9/11 GI Bill, effective on August 1, 2009, the University System of Ohio is taking a proactive step to better serve those who serve our country. The following are components of our state-level initiative, the Ohio GI Promise.

Other Ohio State Veteran Benefits

Burial Benefits
Burial Benefits are available for eligible veterans. (Contact your County Veteran Service Officer)

Medals/Awards and Decorations
Your County Veterans Service Office has forms available and can assist veterans and their families in search of Medals and awards. (Contact your County Veteran Service Officer)

Military Records
Your County Veterans Service Office has forms available and can assist veterans and their families in search of military records and discharges. Also please review links to the left for 'Request for Records'. (Contact your County Veteran Service Officer)

Military/Veteran License Plates
Ohio's Bureau of Motor Vehicles has many military/veteran license plates available to eligible veterans.

Transportation to Medical Appointments
Many of the organizations and County Veterans Service Offices across Ohio free transportation to local VA facilities. (Contact your County Veteran Service Officer)

Updating your Discharge
Your County Veterans Service office has the forms available to request updates to your discharges and can assist you in submitting the form properly. (Contact your County Veteran Service Officer)

Recreational Benefits
Ohio offers the following recreation benefits for qualifying veterans:

- Hunting & Fishing Licenses for qualified veterans
FOR INFORMATION CALL 1-800-WILDLIFE (945-3543)

- Boating Licenses for qualified veterans
FOR INFORMATION CALL 877-426-2837

- Camping at Ohio State Parks
FOR INFORMATION CALL 877-426-2837

Oklahoma State Veteran's Benefits

The state of Oklahoma provides several veteran benefits. This section offers a brief description of each of the following benefits.

- Housing Benefits

- Financial Assistance Benefits

- Employment Benefits

- Other State Veteran Benefits

Oklahoma Veteran Housing Programs

State Veterans Center
The following are state nursing homes located in Oklahoma:

- Ardmore--175 nursing care beds

- Claremore--302 nursing care bgeds

- Clinton--148 nursing care beds--8 domiciliary beds

- Lawton--200 nursing care beds

- Norman--301 nursing care beds

- Sulphur--132 nursing care beds

- Talihina--175 nursing care beds

Visit the Oklahoma Dept. of Veterans Affairs website for contact information and benefits assistance.

Oklahoma Financial Assistance Benefits

Tax Exemption
Tax Exemption for 100% Disabled Veterans for sales tax, excise tax, and ad valorem tax (Spouse included for ad valorem tax only)

Oklahoma Employment Benefits

Veterans Preference
In establishing employment lists of eligible persons for competitive and noncompetitive appointment, certain preferences shall be allowed for veterans honorably discharged from the Armed Forces of the United States.

1. Five points shall be added to the final grade of any person who has passed the examination and has submitted proof of having status as a veteran or unremarried surviving spouse of a veteran.

2. Ten points shall be added to the final grade of any war veteran of the Oklahoma Statutes who has passed the examination and has submitted proof of having a service-connected disability as certified by the Veterans Administration or Agency of the Defense Department within six months of date of application.

3. In addition to the 10 points preference such eligible war veterans who are in receipt of benefits payable at the rate of 30% or more because of the service-connected disability, shall be considered Absolute Preference Veterans. Their names shall be placed at the top of the register, ranked in order of their examination scores. Absolute Preference Veterans shall not be denied employment and passed over for others without showing cause.

Other Oklahoma State Veteran Benefits

Free Hunting and Fishing Permit
Free hunting and fishing permit for legal residents with 60% or more disability.

Emergency/Disaster Financial Assistance Program

Reduced Fee Auto Tags

Visit the Oklahoma Dept. of Veterans Affairs website for contact information and benefits assistance.

The Claims and Benefits Division
The Claims and Benefits Division provides many different services to the veterans and their dependents. The primary function is to assist veterans and their dependents with their claims before the U.S. Department of Veterans Affairs. Claims worked through the Muskogee Claims Office help claimants obtain compensation and pension benefits. Oklahoma Department of Veterans Affairs Service Officers and Claims Officers are accredited with a number of service organizations in order to better represent the claimant with their claims and appeals. The Claims Officers will assist in the appeals process, and if necessary, represent the claimant at a personal hearing before the U.S. Department of Veterans Affairs Hearing Officer. The Muskogee Claims Office handles lifetime hunting & fishing permits, special veterans license plates, and the Financial Assistance Program.

Oregon State Veteran's Benefits

The state of Oregon provides several veteran benefits. This section offers a brief description of each of the following benefits.

- Housing Benefits
- Financial Assistance Benefits
- Employment Benefits
- Education Benefits
- Other State Veteran Benefits
- Oregon Veterans Benefits Website

Oregon Veteran Housing Programs

Oregon Veterans Home Loans
A home loan program for honorably discharged veterans with below market interest
rates. The eligibility for the program expires 30 years after discharge from the U.S. Armed
Forces. ODVA also offers home improvement loans. Toll free information number 1-800-828-
8801.

Oregon Veterans Home
Known as "The place where honor lives." the Oregon Veterans' Home is a skilled nursing care
facility for Oregon veterans, their spouses or surviving spouses, and parents all of whose
children died while serving in the U.S. Armed Forces. Toll free information number 1-800-846-
8460.

Oregon Property Tax Exemption
If you are a disabled veteran or the surviving spouse of a war veteran, you may be entitled to
exempt $15,450 or $18,540 of your homestead property's assessed value from property
taxes.

The exemption amount increases by 3 percent each year. The exemption is first applied to
your home and then to your taxable personal property. If you are an Oregon resident and a
qualifying veteran or that veteran's surviving spouse and live in your home, you may file a
claim and receive the exemption.

Oregon Financial Assistance Programs

Oregon Conservatorship Program
Financial management program for certain veterans their dependents and survivors.
Managing the financial affairs of these protected persons helps meet their current and future
needs.

Oregon Veterans' Emergency Financial Assistance Program (OVEFAP)
When funds are available, this financial assistance program is available for veterans and
their immediate family (spouse, unremarried surviving spouse, child or step child) who are in
need of emergency financial assistance.

Assistance needs includes, but are not limited to:

135

- Emergency or temporary housing and related housing expenses, such as expenses for utilities, insurance, house repairs, rent assistance or food;

- Emergency medical or dental expenses;

- Emergency transportation;

- Expenses related to starting a business, such as business licenses or occupational licenses;

- Temporary income after military discharge; and

- Legal assistance.

NOTE: This program is funded quaterly and often runs out of funds, be sure to contact the ODVA for assistance and to find out if funds are currently available

Oregon Veteran Employment Programs

Oregon Veterans' Employment Preference
Veterans preference in public employment. Additional preference for disabled veterans. Preference points are awarded to eligible veterans seeking employment with all state agencies, and are awarded as follows:

- A five (5) point preference for eligible veterans.

  - Application is made within 15 years of discharge or release from service in the Armed Forces

- A ten (10) point preference for service-connected disabled Veterans.

Application is made throughout the lifetime of the disabled veteran.

Oregon Veterans' Reemployment Rights
Oregon Veterans' are entitled to their old job, seniority, and pay with accrued status upon release of service. Enforced by the United States Department of Labor, Uniformed Services Employment and Reemployment Rights Act (USERRA). USERRA protects all members of the uniformed services from discrimination in employment regardless of whether their uniformed service was in the past, present or future.

Learn more about Oregon Veterans' Reemployment Rights

Oregon Education Assistance Programs

Oregon Educational Aid

The Oregon Department of Veterans' Affairs provides educational benefits for pursuit of approved training courses.

Benefits will be paid for as many months as the veteran spent in active service, up to a maximum of 36 months. Veterans' who qualify for the program are entitled to receive up to $150 per month.   Benefits are paid for classroom instruction, home study courses, and for vocational training from an accredited educational institution.

Note: ODVAs Educational Aid will not be paid if the veteran is currently receiving federal educational benefits under any federal act.

Payment Amounts

- Full-time students are entitled to receive up to $150 per month.
- Part-time students are entitled to receive up to $100 per month.
- School criteria determines full-time and part-time status.

Eligibility Requirements

1. Active duty in the Armed Forces of the U.S. for not less than 90 days; and
2. Released from military service under honorable conditions; and
3. Is a resident of Oregon when applying for State Educational Aid; and
4. Is a citizen of the United States; and
5. Served during the Korean War (June 25, 1950 to January 31, 1955) or after June 30, 1958.

Benefit for Dependents of Deceased, Disabled Oregon Veterans

Oregon's State Legislature passed a law that provides a full-tuition waiver for a bachelor's or master's degree at an Oregon University System institution for children or spouses of servicemembers who died on active duty, became 100 percent disabled in connection with military service, or died as a result of a disability sustained on active duty.
Information on the tuition waiver as well as the application form can be found Oregon University System website under "Featured Documents and Links."

High School Diploma
A school district may issue diplomas under ORS 332.114 to veterans who did not graduate from a high school because they were serving in the Armed Forces.

Other Oregon State Veteran Benefits

Oregon Hunting and Fishing Licenses
A free lifetime Oregon hunting and angling license to service-connected disabled veterans rated 25% or more. Disabled veterans are also eligible for an Oregon Elk tag at a reduced cost. Active members of the armed forces or veterans who retired from the Armed Forces within 12 months of the date of application, may apply to the Oregon Military Department for reimbursement for the cost of a resident annual hunting and angling license.

Oregon State Park Use Permits
Service-connected disabled Veterans and active duty military personnel on leave have free day-use parking and free overnight rental of RV and tent campsites for up to five consecutive days and no more than 10 days total in a calendar month.

Oregon Veteran License Plates
Veterans may purchase a license plate set displaying the word VETERAN for a $10 surcharge in addition to normal fees from a local Oregon Division of Motor Vehicles office. The $10 surcharge goes to the support of the Oregon Veterans' Home. Proof of honorable military service is required. Former POWs, members of the active Oregon National Guard and certain veteran service organization names are available on license plates.

Service-connected disabled veterans qualify for a one time registration fee for motor vehicle registration. These plates do not allow parking in designated disabled parking spaces.

Oregon Public Records
Certified copies of Oregon marriage, death, divorce, and birth records for VA claims purposes are provided free of charge. Also note that county clerks will record veterans' discharge papers (DD Form 214) and provide copies of recorded documents free of charge.

Pennsylvania State Veteran's Benefits

The state of Pennsylvania provides several veteran benefits. This section offers a brief description of each of the following benefits.

- Veteran Housing Benefits
- Veteran Financial Assistance Benefits
- Veteran Employment Benefits
- Veteran and Dependents Education Benefits
- Other State Sponsored Veteran Benefits

Pennsylvania Veteran Housing Programs

State Veterans Homes
The veterans must have served in the Armed Forces of the United States or Pennsylvania military forces, released from service under honorable conditions.

The veteran must be a bona fide resident of the Commonwealth when applying. Spouses and surviving spouses of eligible veterans may also apply. Applications are processed on a "first come, first served" basis.

Pennsylvania Financial Assistance Benefits

Persian Gulf Conflict Veterans' Bonus Program
Pennsylvania voters gave overwhelming approval to funding for the Persian Gulf Conflict Veterans Compensation Program when they voted in the general election on November 7, 2006. This program will provide payments to veterans of Operation Desert Storm and Desert Shield (August 1990 to August 1991). Implementation of the new program will require consideration of regulations and various administrative actions.

Veterans Emergency Assistance
Provides financial aid in an emergency and temporary basis (not to exceed three months in a 12-month period) to veterans, their widows, infant children or dependents who reside in Pennsylvania for the necessities of life (food, dairy, shelter, fuel and clothing). An honorably discharged veteran must have served in the Armed Forces of the United States during

established war service dates or during peacetime hostile fire or terrorist attack as determined by the Department of Military and Veterans Affairs. Upon the recent death of a veteran, his widow or orphan children are eligible provided the veteran would have qualified prior to his/her death.

Real Estate Tax Exemption
Any honorably discharged veteran who is a resident of the Commonwealth shall be exempt from the payment of all real estate taxes levied upon any building, including the land upon which it stands, occupied by him as his principal dwelling, provided that as a result of wartime military service the veteran has a 100% service-connected disability rating by the U.S. Department of Veterans Affairs; that such dwelling is owned by him solely or jointly with his spouse (an estate by the entirety); and that the financial need for the exemption from the payment of real estate taxes has been determined by the State Veterans' Commission. Upon the death of the qualified veteran, the exemption passes on to the unmarried surviving spouse if the financial need can be shown.

Blind Veterans Pension
Provides for a pension of $150.00 per month for a person who served in the military or naval forces of the United States, or women's organization officially connected therewith, who gave the Commonwealth as his/her place of residence when entering the military and while performing duties connected with the service, suffered an injury or incurred a disease which resulted in loss of vision so that the visual acuity with the best correcting lens is 3/60 or 10/200 or equivalent, or less normal vision in the better eye. Less normal vision than 3/60 or 10/200, or equivalent, includes circumstances where the widest diameter of the visual field of the better eye has contracted to such an extent that it subtends an angular distance of not greater than 20?. The term does not include a person separated from the military or naval forces of the United States or a women's organization officially connected therewith under other than honorable conditions.

Paralyzed Veterans Pension
Provides for a pension of $150.00 per month for any person separated under honorable conditions from the Armed Forces of the United States, who gave the Commonwealth of Pennsylvania as his or her place of residence at time of entering the military or naval forces of the United States, and who currently resides in Pennsylvania. Veterans qualify for the pension if they suffered an injury or disease resulting in the loss or loss of use of two or more extremities (arms/hands or legs/feet).

Pennsylvania Education Benefits

Educational Gratuity
Payment of educational gratuities are for children of honorably discharged veterans who have been certified by the U.S. Department of Veterans Affairs as having wartime service-connected disabilities rated as totally and permanently disabled or children of veterans who die or have died of war service-connected disabilities or died in service during a period of war or armed conflict. Children must be between the ages of 16 and 23, living within the Commonwealth five years prior to application and must attend a school within the Commonwealth to be entitled to this educational gratuity.

Rhode Island State Veteran's Benefits

The state of Rhode Island provides veteran benefits. This section offers a brief description of each of the following benefits.

- Rhode Island Veteran's Home
- Rhode Island Veteran's Cemetery
- Rhode Island Veteran's Benefit Counseling

The Rhode Island Veteran's Home
The Rhode Island Veterans Home, a 110-acre complex located on Mount Hope Bay, at 480 Metacom Avenue in Bristol, Rhode Island.

The mission of the home is to provide quality nursing and residential care to those Rhode Island war veterans in need. Social, medical, nursing and rehabilitative services are also provided to veterans and their survivors and/or dependents to improve their physical, emotional and economic well-being.

The Veterans Home consists of 260 nursing care beds in three skilled and semiskilled units and two ambulatory care units and two ambulatory care units with an additional 79 beds..

The Rhode Island Veteran's Cemetery
The Division of Veterans Affairs maintains a dignified and solemn military cemetery on 265 acres in Exeter, Rhode Island. The cemetery serves as a final resting place for Rhode Island Veterans who have served their country honorably during wartime and their eligible dependents. Twenty-year retirees of the Rhode Island National Guard have recently become eligible, as have reserve components of the National Guard and two-year active services personnel with honorable discharges.

Rhode Island Veterans Benefits Counseling
The Rhode Island Veterans Affairs Office offers benefit counseling including a variety of social services to Rhode Island armed forces personnel, veterans, and their dependents who are seeking assistance.

This office processes all applications for admissions to the RI Veterans Home and will conduct home visits, if needed, for those veterans applying for admission. Other services handled by this office include casework, counseling, referral, budget management, and completion of claims (i.e. pensions, compensations, social security).

The Veterans Affairs Office also provides information needed for the admission team at the Rhode Island Veterans Home to assign the proper level of nursing care to the veterans it serves. In addition, staff at the Veterans Affairs Office work with all state veteran services organizations to assist veterans with their requests for services.

South Carolina State Veteran's Benefits

The state of South Carolina provides several veteran benefits. This section offers a brief description of each of the following benefits.

- Veteran Housing Benefits
- Veteran and Active Duty Financial Assistance Benefits
- Veteran Employment Benefits
- Veteran Dependent Education Benefits
- Other State Sponsored Veteran Benefits

South Carolina Veteran Housing Programs

Specially Adapted Housing
Provides for the exemption of state, county, and municipal taxes on the residence of veterans who have lost the use of their lower extremities or who has paralysis of one lateral half of the body resulting from injury to the motor centers of the brain.

State Veterans Nursing Homes
There are two facilities in South Carolina: the E. Roy Stone Jr., Pavilion, which is located in Columbia, and the Richard Michael Campbell Veterans Nursing Home in Anderson, S.C.

Admission to these facilities is limited to veterans who have been separated from the U.S. Armed Forces under honorable conditions and qualify as South Carolina residents who are in need of skilled or intermediate nursing home care.

South Carolina Financial Assistance Benefits

Admissions Tax Exemption
Provides for the exemption of admissions taxes to athletic contests in which junior American Legion athletic teams are participants unless the proceeds are given to individual players in the form of salary or otherwise.

Income Tax Exemption on Military Retirement Pay
Any person retired from the uniformed services or their surviving spouse, shall be allowed an exemption from the S.C. State Income Tax of $3,000 until age 65. At age 65 $10,000 of retirement pay is exempt.

Property Taxes - Homestead Exemption
All persons who have been declared permanently and totally disabled by the Social Security Administration, U.S. Department of Veterans Affairs, other state or federal agencies, are eligible for a homestead exemption in an amount set by the General Assembly. This also applies to persons over age 65.

Property Tax Exemption
Provides that the dwelling house in which a veteran resides who has been rated as permanently and totally disabled by the U.S. Department of Veterans Affairs may be tax exempt. The tax exemption may be transferred when purchasing another dwelling.

Tax Exemption for Compensation, Pension, Disability Retirement Pay and VA Payments
Provides that federal tax exempt moneys received from pension or compensation provided by the U.S. Department of Veterans Affairs, or disability pay from the Armed Forces will not be included in SC tax.

Parking Fee Exemption
Provides for an exemption of municipal parking meter fees when a veteran's vehicle bears a disabled veteran ("V" tag), Purple Heart or Medal of Honor license plate.

Active Duty Pay Relevant to the SC Department of Revenue & Taxation
Non-resident armed services personnel who are legal residents of other States stationed within South Carolina by virtue of military orders, are not subject to South Carolina income tax on their service pay. They are, however, subject to tax on any other income earned in South Carolina by spouses of service personnel.

South Carolina Employment Benefits

Veterans Preference
Preference will be granted to eligible members for employment and/or an appointment in public departments or public works operating on a merit system.
Eligible members:

- Must be Honorably discharged from the Armed Forces of the U.S.

- Must possess the skills and knowledge required for the position involved.

Veterans Reemployment Rights
Employees of the State/any political subdivision thereof, on or after June 25, 1950 has been, or will be, commissioned, enlisted/selected for service in the Armed Forces of the U.S. shall be entitled to a leave of absence from his/her duties as an employee of the State/any political subdivision thereof, without loss of seniority or efficiency or register rating.

South Carolina Education Benefits

Education Assistance (Fee tuition for certain veteran's children)
Provides for free tuition to the children of certain war veterans attending South Carolina state supported colleges and universities as well as state supported post high school technical education institutions. Certain residency requirements apply.

Other South Carolina State Veteran Benefits

Credit of State Retirement for Military Service
A person leaving employment with the State for military duty, may continue with the State's Retirement Program if he/she continues to make payments based on the salary he/she was receiving when employed by the State.

An employee of the State with two or more years of credited service with the South Carolina Retirement System may also purchase additional credit, up to six years, for military service towards his/her State retirement.

Free Hunting & Fishing Licenses
Provides for free hunting/fishing license to veterans who are totally disabled. License must be applied for directly from SC Department of Natural Resources showing proof of disability.

State Parks Totally Disabled Persons
Provides that any South Carolina resident who is a permanently and totally disabled veteran may enter any state park at a reduced rate upon presentation of supporting disability documentation. The veteran may also apply for a reduced fee "Palmetto Passport." Certain services may require an additional fee.

Special License Plates
Upon establishing proof of eligibility to entitlement, the S.C. Department of Public Safety may issue special motor vehicle license plates to the following:

- National Guard
- National Guard Retirees
- Purple Heart Recipients
- Disabled Veterans
- U.S. Armed Forces Retirees
- Ex-Prisoners of War
- Medal of Honor Recipients
- Pearl Harbor Survivors
- Normandy Invasion Survivors
- Marine Corps League

Presentation of the State Flag to Families of Deceased Members of the South Carolina National Guard
Provides that the State Adjutant General's Office shall present to the family of each deceased member of the South Carolina National Guard a flag of the State of South Carolina, appropriate for use as a burial flag, upon application of a member of the family of the deceased.

Recording of Discharges
A certified copy of the recorded discharge may be obtained upon request. Any person desiring a certified copy of any discharge or certificate of lost discharge, may apply to the County Clerk of Court or the County Veterans Affairs Officer in which the discharge or certificate of lost discharge is registered and shall be furnished a certified copy. Fees for furnishing a certified copy of discharge or DD Form 214 may be established by each county, but may not exceed fifty cents.

Marriage, Birth, Death and Divorce Verification
Provides for the verification of marriage, birth, death, and divorce records without cost when

such is required by the U.S. Department of Veterans Affairs, the S.C. Division of Veterans Affairs, the County Veterans Affairs Offices, or any out of state Veterans Affairs entities.

South Dakota State Veteran's Benefits

The state of South Dakota provides several veteran benefits. This section offers a brief description of each of the following benefits.

- Veteran Housing Benefits:
- Veteran Financial Assistance Benefits
- Veteran Education Benefits
- Other State Sponsored Veteran Benefits

South Dakota Veteran Housing Programs

State Veterans Homes
To provide a quality living environment, along with adequate medical support, in an independent living and long-term care setting for eligible South Dakota veterans and their spouses, widows, or widowers; and, to provide administration, maintenance, management, medical care, and other services necessary to meet or exceed state and federal requirements.

South Dakota Financial Assistance Programs

Emergency Loan Fund for Veterans and Their Dependents
An interest free loan of up to $500 may be made, to veterans or a veteran's dependents, if financial relief is required for any emergency need.

The amount loaned must be repaid within two years. To qualify, the veteran must meet the definition of a veteran (SDCL 33-17-1 & 33-17-2) and must have been a legal resident of South Dakota at the time of entry into service or for at least one year immediately prior to application.

Property Tax Exemption for Veterans and Their Widow or Widower
Dwellings or parts of multiple family dwellings which are specifically designed for use by paraplegics as wheelchair homes and which are owned and occupied by veterans with the loss, or loss of use, of both lower extremities, or by the unremarried widow or widower of such veteran, are exempt from taxation.
The dwelling must be owned and occupied by the veteran for one full calendar year before the exemption becomes effective. For purposes of this statute, the term "dwelling" generally means real estate in an amount not to exceed one acre upon which the building is located.

In addition veterans that have been rated as permanently and totally disabled as the result of a service connected disability may be eligible for up to $100,000 of their property value to be exempt from property taxes.

Property Tax Refund for Aged and Disabled Persons
Certain low income property owners are eligible for a property tax refund and should check with their county treasurer for details and assistance in making application. To qualify the following conditions must be met:

1. The head of the household must be sixty-five years of age, or older, or shall be disabled prior to January first of the year in which taxes are levied;

2. The applicant must have owned the property for at least three years or, have been a resident of this state at least five years if not qualified under the three year ownership criteria.

Learn more about the Property Tax Refund

Sales Tax Refund for Certain Elderly and Disabled Persons
Certain low income persons who are sixty-five, or older, or who are disabled, may qualify for a sales tax refund. Applicants should check with their county treasurer for details and assistance.

Note: No individual may receive both a property tax and sales tax refund in the same year.

South Dakota Veterans Bonuses

South Dakota currently offers a bonus of up to $500 for current or former eligible members of the Armed Forces who were legal residents of the state for no less than six months immediately preceding their period of active duty and who meet certain criteria during one or more of the following periods:

- August 2, 1990 to March 3, 1991 – All active service counts for payment.

- March 4, 1991 to December 31, 1992 – Only service in a hostile area qualifying for the Southwest Asia Service Medal counts for payment.

- January 1, 1993 to September 10, 2001 – Only service in a hostile area qualifying for any United States campaign or service medal awarded for combat operations against hostile forces counts for payment.

- September 11, 2001 to a date to be determined – [OIF/OEF] All active service counts for payment.

Veterans living outside of South Dakota may obtain an application by email at john.fette@state.sd.us. Please include your branch of the military and dates of service. Veterans may also request an application and instructions by writing SD Veterans Bonus, 500 E. Capitol, Pierre, SD 57501 or by calling 605-773-7251.

Veterans living in South Dakota may apply through the nearest County or Tribal Veterans Service Officer.

South Dakota Education Assistance Programs

Free Tuition for Veterans
Certain veterans are eligible to take undergraduate courses at a state university without the payment of tuition provided they are not eligible for educational payments under the GI Bill or

any other federal educational program.

Eligible veterans may receive one month of free tuition for each month of "qualifying service" with a minimum of one, up to a maximum of four, academic years. Qualifying service is defined as: the amount of time served on active duty between the beginning and ending dates of the particular period of conflict or hostilities during which the veteran earned eligibility for this program.

Free Tuition for Children of Veterans Who Die During Service
Children who are under the age of 25, are residents of South Dakota, and whose mother or father was killed in action or died of other causes while on active duty, are eligible for free tuition at a state supported school, if the deceased parent was a bona-fide resident of this state for at least six months immediately preceding entry into active service.

SDDVA form E-12 "Application for Free Tuition at State Supported Institutions" is available at the schools' financial aids, veterans representative or registrars offices or, they can be obtained from the Division of Veterans Affairs.

Free Tuition for Dependents of POW's and MIA's
Children and spouses of prisoners of war, or of persons listed as missing in action, are entitled to attend a state supported school without the payment of tuition or mandatory fees provided they are not eligible for equal or greater federal benefits.

SDDVA form E-12 "Application for Free Tuition at State Supported Institutions" is available at the schools' financial aids, veterans representative or registrars offices or, they can be obtained from the Division of Veterans Affairs.

Reduced Tuition for South Dakota National Guardmembers
Guard members, who meet the requirements for admission, are eligible for a fifty percent reduction in undergraduate tuition charges at any state supported school for up to a maximum of four academic years or one program of study, approved by the state Board of Education, at any state vocational school upon payment of fifty percent of the tuition charges.

The receipt of federal educational benefits does not affect eligibility for this program.

Other South Dakota State Veteran Benefits

Free Certified Copies of Veterans Records
South Dakota counties may not charge for certified copies of birth, death, marriage, adoption, divorce, guardianship or conservatorship papers when such records are required in support of a claim against any agency of the federal or state government by, or on behalf of, a servicemember or veteran, or the spouse, surviving spouse or dependents of a servicemember or veteran.

Burial Allowance for Veterans, Wives or Widows
A payment of up to $100 may be paid by the state to help defray the burial and funeral expenses of any honorably discharged veteran or the wife, widow or widower of a veteran when the estate, or immediate family, of the deceased is lacking in funds to pay the expenses. The veteran must have been a citizen of the United States for one year preceding

entrance into military service or one year preceding the death. This payment CANNOT be made to another unit of government. The surviving spouse, or relatives, must furnish an affidavit to the C/TVSO that sufficient funds are not available for payment of the expenses.

Headstone Setting Fee
The state will pay $40 towards the cost of setting a government headstone or marker at the grave of a veteran who was a resident of this state for one year preceding entrance into the military service or one year preceding death.

Special License Plates
A resident veteran owner of a motor vehicle who has a valid South Dakota driver's license and who signs an affidavit attesting to the fact that he or she is an honorably discharged veteran having served on active duty in the armed forces of the United States, may apply for Veteran plates. The fee for the special plates is $10.00 per set, in addition to registration fees. A $5.00 mailing fee required for each set of license plates to be mailed.

No special plate renewal fee is charged, but registration fees apply.

The following plates are available to eligible persons:

- Disabled Veteran Plate
- Prisoner of War Plate
- Pearl Harbor Survivor Plate
- Purple Heart Plate

Hunting and Fishing Cards for Disabled Veterans
Certain resident veterans may receive a hunting and fishing card which is valid for four years. Upon purchase of an annual basic game and fish license, the card becomes the equivalency of a resident fishing license, small game stamp and habitat stamp until the expiration of the basic game and fish license. To qualify the veteran must:

1. be rated as totally disabled from service connected injuries OR,
2. be in receipt of the VA "K" award OR,
3. have been held as a Prisoner of War OR,
4. be in receipt of Social Security benefits because of a total disability.

Free Admission and Reduced Camping Fees for Veterans
Certain resident veterans may obtain free admission to any South Dakota state park and are eligible for a fifty percent discount on any camping fee or associated electrical fee. To qualify the veteran must:

1. be totally disabled from service connected disabilities or,
2. be in receipt of the VA "K" award OR,
3. have been held as a Prisoner of War.

Application forms may be obtained from the local park manager or through the Game, Fish and Parks office in Pierre.

Special Provisions for Handicapped Hunters
Individuals who are missing an upper limb, or are physically incapable of using an upper limb or who are confined to a wheelchair may use a crossbow to take game birds and animals once they have obtained a disabled hunter permit.

A legally blind, legally licensed individual who possesses a disabled hunter permit and who is physically present and participating in the hunt may claim game birds and animals taken by a designated hunter in accordance with the license or licenses possessed by the handicapped hunter.

Applications are obtained from the Game, Fish and Parks office in Pierre or from a game warden.

Tennessee State Veteran's Benefits

The state of Tennessee provides several veteran benefits. This section offers a brief description of each of the following benefits.

- Veteran Housing Benefits
- Veteran Employment Benefits
- Other State Veteran Benefits

Tennessee Veteran Housing Programs

State Veterans Homes
Tennessee offers two state veteran homes who's goal is to provide veterans with the best health care in an environment which is pleasant and enjoyable; to provide a safe, warm and happy home for our veterans.

To treat our veterans with the dignity and respect they deserve.

Property Tax Relief
Property tax relief for combat related 100% totally disabled veterans and/or their surviving spouses.

Tennessee Veteran Employment Programs

Employment Programs
The following employment benefits are available in Tennessee:

- Veterans preference in State employment
- Credit for military service in State employment
- Reemployment rights of public employees

Other Tennessee State Veteran Benefits

State Veterans Cemeteries
Tennesse offers eligible veterans their choice of state veteran cemeteries in Knoxville, Memphis, and Nashville.

Free License Plates
Free license plates for 100% service connected disabled veterans, Ex-POW's, and recipients of MOH, DSC, NC or AFC.

Free Hunting and Fishing Licenses
Free hunting and fishing licenses for Veterans with 30% or more war service connected disabilities, after an initial one time fee of $10.

Parking Privileges
Parking privileges for free license plate holders.

Motor Vehicle Privilege Tax Exemption
Motor vehicle privilege tax exemption for 100% disabled veterans.

Special/Memorial License Plates
Special/Memorial license plates for certain veterans.

No-Fee Registration of Discharges
Registration of discharges by county registrar at no fee

Texas State Veteran's Benefits

The state of Texas provides several veteran benefits. This section offers a brief description of each of the following benefits.

- Veteran Housing Benefits
- Veteran Financial Assistance Benefits
- Veteran Education Benefits
- Veteran Employment Benefits
- Other State Sponsored Veteran Benefits

Texas Veteran Housing Programs

Texas Veterans Land Board Programs
The Texas Veterans Land Board (VLB), a division of the Texas General Land Office, administers three veterans' loan programs:

The Land Loan Program, Veterans Housing Assistance Purchase Program, and the Veterans

149

Home Improvement Loan Program. We have provided additional information on our site and a link to the VLB website.

Texas Financial Assistance Programs

Tax Exemption for Veterans
Disabled veterans who meet certain requirements, their surviving spouses and the spouses and minor children of a person who dies on active duty in the U.S. Armed Forces are eligible for property tax exemptions on the appraised value of their property. The exemption is mandatory and applies to taxes levied by all taxing authorities in the State. A veteran, whose service-connected disabilities are rated less than 10% by the Department of Veterans Affairs, or a branch of the Armed Forces, is not entitled to a property tax exemption.

Texas State Veteran Education Benefits

The Hazlewood Act
Wartime veterans who were legal residents of Texas at the time they entered military service, and Home of Record is listed as Texas on the DD214, are entitled to a waiver of tuition and some fees at State-supported/public (taxpayer supported) colleges and universities. This benefit is also available to children of Texas servicemen and women who died or were killed in military service, and to children of Texas military personnel who are shown to be missing in action or prisoners of war. Also eligible are children of members of the Texas National Guard or the Texas Air National Guard killed since January 1, 1946, while on active duty either in service of Texas or the United States.

Texas Veteran Employment Programs

Veterans Preference
Wartime veterans have preference in employment with State agencies or offices, as do widows and children of those killed on active duty. State agencies must practice veterans' preference until they have reached 40% veteran employment. Non-retired veterans who are employed by the State of Texas are entitled to claim their active duty military time toward retirement, provided they present a proper request and pay to the Retirement System the specified amount of retirement contribution for up to 60 months' military credit. Such contribution is paid at the rate which was applicable at the time the employed veteran first was covered by the state Retirement System, plus any accrued interest. We have provided a link to the the State Law regarding veterans' preference laws.

Additionally, a veteran is entitled to reemployment rights with his last employer when he is released from the Armed Forces of the United States, providing his absence is not longer than four years. The right of reemployment is available regardless of whether the veteran was, prior to service, employed by the State, county or city government, or by private industry. Reemployment rights of veterans are now provided by both State and Federal laws. We have provided a link to the State Law regarding reemployment rights.

Other Texas State Veteran Benefits

Texas State Cemetery Program
In the November 2001 statewide elections, voters overwhelmingly approved Proposition 7, a constitutional amendment that authorized the creation of up to seven state cemeteries for veterans and their eligible dependents. The cemeteries will be built and operated through a partnership between the Texas Veterans Land Board (VLB) and the U.S. Department of Veterans Affairs (USDVA). The USDVA will fund up to 100 percent of the construction and equipment costs. The state will own and operate the cemeteries and fund most of the cost of operations.

No-Cost Medical Records
Under the Health and Safety Code, Chapter 161.201 Subchapter M, Medical or Mental Health Records, Texas veterans are eligible for no cost medical records when they are obtained to file a claim for a disability against the U.S. Department of Veterans Affairs (USDVA). The health care provider or health care facility is not required to provide more than one complete record for the patient or former patient without charge. Also, it should be noted, that some medical facilities will charge a small administrative fee for obtaining the records.

Free Drivers License for Disabled Veterans
Under Texas Transportation Code Title 7, Chapter 521, Section 521.426, Texas drivers licenses may be furnished free of charge to veterans who have service-connected disabilities rated 60% or more by the VA or by a branch of the Armed Forces of the U.S. Application must be made prior to the time present drivers license expires. Application forms may be obtained from Department of Public Safety's license examining offices located throughout the State. We have provided a link to the to the Texas Department of Public Safety's Drivers License information website. Application forms should be completed by the veteran and forwarded to the VA for verification of service-connected rating of 60% or more. If a veteran was disability-retired from military service and has no VA claim file, proof of disability must come from their respective branch of military service.

Fishing and Hunting Licenses for Disabled Veterans
Disabled veterans are eligible for special hunting and fishing licenses, at a reduced cost. A disabled veteran of the Armed Forces of the United States is one who has a service-connected disability, as defined by the Department of Veterans Affairs, consisting of the loss of use of a lower extremity or of a disability rating of 60% or more, and who is receiving compensation from the United States for the disability. A resident veteran as described in the law may hunt wild turkey and deer without a resident hunting license if he has acquired a resident exemption hunting license.

Free Park Admission for Disabled Veterans
Free admission to Texas State Parks is available to any veteran who has a service-connected disability, which is rated 60% or more by VA, or a service-connected disability, which has resulted in the loss of a lower extremity. Application may be made at the headquarters office of any Texas State park by providing satisfactory evidence of service-connected disability. If such evidence is not readily available, it can be obtained from the VA regional office where the claims folder is located. The Texas State Parklands Passport is available to any veteran who

meets the disability requirements, whether or not he or she resides in Texas. The Passport provides only free admission to the State parks, and does not exempt anyone from payment of other charges, such as camping fees, etc.

Free Recording of Discharges
Under Texas State law, Local Government Code Sec. 0192.002, the County Clerk in each County is required to record, free of charge, the official discharge of each veteran who served in the Armed Forces of the United States of America. This free service is very important as it provides veterans with a ready source from which they can obtain a certified copy of their discharge whenever it is needed. It is the veteran's responsibility to have the DD214 or Discharge recorded. Please also note that if you do record your DD214 with the County Clerk, it then becomes a public record. See "Safeguard Your Discharge (DD214)" in MS Word or Acrobat PDF. Also note that the Texas Veterans Commission does not keep a record of your DD214 or Discharge.

Special License Plates
Disabled Veterans, Former Prisoners of War, Pearl Harbor Survivors, Purple Heart and Medal of Honor plates are among the special license plates available to eligible veterans and their survivors for personal use on their automobile or light commercial vehicle of one ton or less. Disabled veterans must have a service-connected disability rating of 50% or more or 40% due to amputation of a lower extremity. Former prisoners of war are eligible if they were captured or incarcerated by an enemy of the United States during a period of conflict with the United States and at the time of the capture, were citizens of the United States. Eligibility is for both former members of the Armed Forces and civilian U.S. citizens who were captured by an enemy of our government. For further information, contact either the nearest vehicle title registration office or your county tax office.

Utah State Veteran's Benefits

The state of Utah provides several veteran benefits. This section offers a brief description of each of the following benefits.

- Veteran Housing Benefits
- Employment Benefits
- Education Benefits
- Other State Veteran Benefits

Utah Veteran Housing and Tax Programs

Property Tax Abatement
A Utah permanent place-of-residence property tax exemption equivalent to the military service-connected disability rating percentage is provided for disabled veterans or for their unremarried widows or minor orphans.

Veteran's disability rating must be at least 10%. The maximum property tax exemption, rated at 100% military service-connected disability, is $219.64. To figure out how much your tax abatement will be multiply your percentage of disability by 219,164. Example: 10% disability X

206,214 = $21,916.40 tax abatement.

To apply for Utah Disabled Veterans Property Tax Exemption, request VA Form 20-5455 from U.S. Dept. of Veterans Affairs (VA) at 1-800-827-1000, then file VA Form 20-5455, along with a copy of the veteran's U.S. Military active duty release/discharge certificate or other satisfactory evidence of eligible military service, and the tax exemption application, on or before September 1, to the applicable county treasurer, tax assessor or clerk/recorder located in the county courthouse or county government building of each county seat.

All property must be on record as of January 1st of the year you wish to file. However, a recent change allows qualified widows and orphans an exemption to that rule.

Disabled veterans are only be required to file for property tax abatement one time. After the initial filing it will automatically renew each year although the counties may require recertification of home address. However, veterans will have to re-file if all or a portion of their abatement is used towards tangible personal property (i.e. vehicles), if their service-connected disability percentage changes, the veteran dies, sales the property or no longer claims that property as their primary place of residence. (Utah Code 59-2-1104 & 1105)

Utah Veteran Employment Programs

Veterans Job Representatives
Local Veterans Employment Representatives (LVER) and Disabled Veterans Outreach Person (DVOP) are located statewide in the larger employment offices of the Utah Dept. of Workforce Services. They provide intensive employment related services for targeted veterans: referral to job opportunities, resume writing, referral letters, veteran's preference, employment counseling, etc.

Veterans Job Preference
Eligible veterans or un-remarried spouses are granted either 5 or 10 points, as applicable, for employment preference, added to the results of any written &/or oral exam or other related qualifying technique, by any Utah government entity (state, county, municipality, special district or other political subdivision or administration.) The U.S. Dept. of Labor will protect the veteran's rights to the Veterans Job Preference.

Veterans Hiring Priority
Any officers, agents or representatives of the state, or any contractor performing work for Utah state government, who willfully fails to hire a military veteran shall be guilty of a misdemeanor.

Utah Veteran Education Assistance Programs

Veterans Upward Bound
VUB is funded by the Department of Education and sponsored by Weber State University. VUB provides a valuable service by assisting veterans in obtaining admission to post-secondary schools. Instruction and tutoring are provided free of charge to veterans in math, English and basic computer applications. The services are provided to veterans in Salt Lake, Davis and Weber Counties.

Tuition Waiver for Purple Heart Recipients

Utah public institutions of higher learning are required to waive the tuition of a Utah resident admitted to an undergraduate program of study leading to a degree or certificate, if the student is a recipient of a Purple Heart. Recent changes have expanded this benefit to include a Masters Degree.

Scott B Lundell Tuition Waiver for Military Members' Surviving Dependents
This Bill waives the undergraduate tuition at state institutions of higher education for surviving dependents of Utah resident military members killed in the line of duty after 9/11/2001. The waiver in this section does not apply to fees, books, or housing expenses. The Utah Department of Veterans Affairs is the administering agency for this benefit. Call 1-800-894-9497 or (801) 326-2372 for information on how to use this benefit.

Honorary High School Diplomas
Veterans from WWII, Korea and Vietnam who left High School for military service are eligible to receive Honorary High School Diplomas from the school they left. Contact the local school district for information on how to receive the diploma.

Other Utah State Veteran Benefits

Drivers License Privileges
Driver licenses possessed by persons on U.S. military active duty shall be valid 90 days after active duty discharge, unless driver licenses are suspended or revoked for cause by a police department or other judicial entity.

Veterans License Plates
Utah veterans license plates may be purchased for an initial $25.00 contribution to the Utah State Division of Veterans Affairs plus a $10.00 plate transfer fee, in addition to normal vehicle registration and property tax fees. Plates can be purchased at any Utah Department of Motor Vehicle office. There will also be a yearly $10.00 renewal fee. Proceeds from the sale and renewal of these plates help fund veteran programs within the state. Utah veteran's license plates display colored decal emblems of the U.S. military branch in which served (Air Force, Army, Coast Guard, Navy, Marines as well as the American Legion) and are further inscribed "UTAH HONORS VETERANS". Utah special group license plates for Purple Heart recipients, Pearl Harbor Survivors or former POW's are exempt of application and renewal fees: however, regular registration and property tax fees still must be paid. Proper evidence to present for special group plates includes Military Order of the Purple Heart or Pearl Harbor Survivors Association membership cards, or DD-214 (& equivalent WD AGO 5355) military discharge certificates. You need not wait until renewal time to purchase the license plates.

Purple Heart Fee Exemption
Recipients of a Purple Heart is exempt from paying the following motor vehicle license and registration fees: automobile driver education fee; motor vehicle registration fee; license plate issuance fees; uninsured motorist identification fee; and local option transportation corridor preservation fee. The only fee due is property tax or age-based fee.

Utah State Division of Veterans Affairs
The Utah State Division of Veterans Affairs is located at 550 Foothill Dr. Suite #202, Salt Lake City, Utah 84113 (the corner of Wasatch & Foothill) on the VA Medical Center Campus. The mission of the office is to provide counsel, assist veterans and their dependents with VA

claims processing, establish veterans' rights to state and federal benefits and to provide information and advisory services. Veteran service officers under contract provide an outreach assistance program to rural Utah veterans, in conjunction with the Utah State Division of Veterans Affairs. U.S. active duty military service discharge certificates (DD-214's) are on file in the office for veterans discharged after 1980. DD-214's are only on file for veterans with Utah residency or with a Utah forwarding address at the time of release from active duty.

Utah State Veterans Nursing Home
The first Utah State Veterans Nursing Home, located on the Salt Lake City VA Medical Center Campus, address, 700 Foothill Drive, SLC, UT. 84113-1104, was dedicated on 22 April 1998 and became operational in May 1998. Quality nursing and health care services are provided for Utah veterans with U.S. military service during peacetime or wartime. While wartime service is not a requirement for admission to the nursing home, wartime veterans with one day or more of wartime service, as recognized by state and federal laws, have top priority. A veteran's spouse or surviving spouse may also qualify for admittance to the Utah State Veterans Nursing Home, providing the marriage to the veteran occurred at least one year before the application. Note: The Utah Legislature has authorized a $4,500,000 bond to construct a veterans nursing home in Ogden. The bond will be repealed on December 31, 2008 if the VA's portion of the funding remains unavailable.

Utah State Veterans Cemetery & Memorial Park
Located at 17111 Camp Williams Road in Bluffdale. This states veteran's cemetery generally follows the eligibility requirements of VA National Cemetery System, including: any U.S. Armed Forces active personnel dying while performing duty or after having served during wartime. Reservist and National Guard retired personnel with 20 years of service are eligible for burial also. Surviving spouses and dependent children also are eligible to be buried in the Utah State Veterans Cemetery & Memorial Park, under rules established by the state of Utah. Authorized in 1988 by act of the Utah State Legislature, dedication occurred on Memorial Day, 1990. Veterans are not to be buried in any portion of any cemetery or burial ground used for paupers; cities, towns, counties or other political subdivisions of the state of Utah may provide proper sites for burial of veterans.

Military Discharge Records
Utah State Archives has military discharge records for Utah (ACTIVE DUTY) veterans from the territorial times, World War II and the Korean War. Utah State Archives will provide a copy of U.S. military discharge records on file free of charge. The Utah State Division of Veterans Affairs has active duty only U.S. military service DD-214's for Utah Veterans from 1980 to the current year. DD-214 certified copies are provided free of charge; toll free 1-800-894-9497. The Utah National Guard Headquarters in Draper Utah maintains file copies of National Guard Bureau record of separation certificates (NGB 22's) for completed service in the Utah Army National Guard & Utah Air National Guard (1950-present). NGB 22 certified copies are free of charge. NOTE: For many years, veterans were encouraged to place their DD-214 on file with their local county recorders office. We no longer recommend this practice because of issues with identity theft.

Free Use of Armories

Organizations of war veterans are entitled to have free use of state of Utah armories as meeting places, provided such use shall not interfere with the use of armories by the National Guard or organized militia of Utah.

Fishing License Privileges
Utah Disabled Veteran Fishing Licenses are available for Veterans, free of charge, from the Utah Division of Wildlife Resources. To qualify a Veteran must have obvious physical handicaps, such as, permanently confined to a wheelchair, paraplegic, minus at least one limb, permanently requiring crutches or blind.

Special Fun Tags
Free admission to most of the 41 state-controlled parks, campgrounds and other recreation areas throughout Utah. Effective July 1,2009, the new policy now allows Utah veterans to receive a special Fun Tag, free of charge, if they are:

1. Legally Blind, which is defined as vision of 20/200 or less in the better eye with best correction, or a field restriction of 20 degrees of less in both eyes; or

2. Non-Ambulatory, which is defined as being permanently confined to a wheelchair or the use of a cane, crutches or mobility device, or who has lost either or both lower extremities.

Special Fun Tag allows dayuse access to most Utah state parks, but does not include This Is The Place Heritage Park and does not cover the $2 Davis County Causeway Fee at Antelope Island State Park. The Special Fun Tag does not apply to camping or other special fees. Please call the State Parks and Recreation office at (801) 538-7220 or toll free at 1-877-UTPARKS to have an application mailed to you or log on to www.stateparks.utah.gov to download.

Applications can be mailed or faxed to (801) 538-7378.

Bus / Trax Reduced Fare Cards
Greatly discounted fares (65% reduced) to ride Utah Transit Authority (UTA) busses and TRAX light rail system are available for veterans meeting one of the following criteria: Forty percent (40%) or greater military service-connected disability rating by VA, in receipt of VA non-service connected pension or regardless of disability rating for veterans & others with transportation disabilities that cause either difficulty boarding or getting off a bus/light rail system, difficulty standing in a moving bus/light rail system, difficulty reading bus/light rail system schedules & understanding information signs, difficulty hearing announcements by bus/light rail system, or difficulty hearing announcements by bus/light rail systems operators.

Persons receiving Social Security Disability benefits, SSI, or Medicare also my get UTA Reduced Fare Cards. Elderly persons age 65 and over qualify for Senior Passes at the same price as Reduced Fare Cards. To obtain UTA Reduced Fare Cards 1. Go to either UTA location at 24 West 100 South or 3600 S 700 W in SLC, 2. Complete UTA Reduced Fare Card application form, 3. Present evidence (a VA letter verifying service connected disability rating or non service connected pension. 4. Pay for UTA photo identification to incorporate on UTA Reduced Fare Card.

Vermont State Veteran's Benefits

The state of Vermont provides several veteran benefits. This section offers a brief description of each of the following benefits.

- Housing Benefits
- Financial Assistance Benefits
- Education Benefits
- Other State Veteran Benefits

Vermont Veteran Housing Programs

Vermont Veterans' Home
Veterans, their spouses, and some dependents and parents may be eligible to live in the Vermont Veterans Home.

The home offers a complete range of specialized health care services. Goals focus on dignity, independence, and the highest quality of life for each resident.

Financial Assistance Programs
The Office of Veterans Affairs provides emergency financial assistance to veterans and their dependents by providing a one-time payment. Applications are processed over the phone or in person. Applicants will need to provide detailed information on their income and expenses to apply.

Vermont War Bonus
The War Bonus is a program that dates back to the War of 1812. It was started to reimburse soldiers for the use of their weapons, horse, etc. during their military duty. Since then, veterans who served during war-time have been eligible, with the last payments made to Vietnam Era veterans. The bonus pays $10 per month of service, to a maximum of $120. Our office still accepts applications from Vietnam Veterans, and an extremely limited amount of funds are still available.

Vermont Veteran Employment Programs

Vermont Employment and Training Assistance
Each State Department of Labor Career Resource Center has professionals who are trained to assist veterans in finding work or job training. They are extremely knowledgeable about veterans' benefits and can refer veterans to the state and federal programs designed to meet their needs. Your local phonebook will have the number of the closest office. When you call, tell them you're a veteran. The link to the left will provide a directory of these professionals in the state.

Vermont Veteran Education Assistance

High School Diplomas for WWII and Korean War Era Veterans
Veterans of the World War II and Korean War Eras who do not have a high school diploma

may be eligible to receive one from a Vermont high school. Applications are verified by the Office of Veterans Affairs, and the diplomas are issued by a secondary school picked by the veteran.

Other Vermont State Veteran Benefits

Veteran Advocacy
The application process for veterans benefits can be confusing and intimidating. If you would like someone to work for you to help make sure you receive the state and federal benefits you and your family deserve, contact our Veteran Service Officer, Mr. Richard Reed. He is a trained and certified professional veterans' advocate who will work on your behalf for no fee.

Discharge Records
The Office of Veterans Affairs maintains copies of active duty discharge records for most veterans who entered the service from Vermont. We help veterans locate their records, will store copies of their records, and will make certified copies of records...all free of charge. Because of the federal Privacy Act, we need to have your request for your discharge in writing. You can come to our office, mail a request, or fax a request. Although we have a Records Request Form, you don't have to use it. If you don't want to use the form, just send us a letter requesting a copy of the discharge (it doesn't have to be typed) with the veteran's name, Social Security Number, date of birth, and approximate dates of service. Make sure to sign the letter and include the address you would like the discharge mailed to. We only release the discharge to the veteran, or the veteran's next of kin if the veteran is deceased.

If the requestor is the next of kin, please provide the veteran's date of death and the relationship to the veteran. Requests can be faxed or mailed...sorry, we can't take Email requests for records. If we don't have your discharge, you can request it from the state you entered the military from or from the National Personnel Records Center. If you need a full copy of your records, to include your medical records, you would need to get them from the records center. Requests from them take a minimum of two months.

Vermont Veterans Memorial Cemetery
The Vermont Veterans Memorial Cemetery is located in Randolph Center. It provides veterans with a resting-place that honors their service at a cost lower than a commercial cemetery. In addition, certain family members may also be buried with the veteran. Applicants can choose from government markers or custom made commercial markers.

Vermont Veterans License Plates
Veterans can receive a Vermont Veterans License Plate when they register their vehicle. Veterans can have a Vermont Veterans License Plate on each of their cars. The Department of Motor Vehicles will charge $10 the first time a vehicle is registered with the plate. Of this fee, $5 goes towards the Office of Veterans Affairs to fund their activities.

Hunting and Fishing Licenses; Green Mountain Pass
Veterans with a Department of Veterans Affairs Service Connected Disability rating of 100% can receive a free lifetime hunting and fishing license. They can also receive a free Green Mountain Pass, which provides free access to state parks. For the hunting and fishing license, you will need to obtain a verification letter from the White River Junction Benefits Office (1-800-827-1000). Submit the verification letter with a standard license application and send it to the Fish and Wildlife Department in Waterbury.

Vermont Medals
Veterans who entered the military when they were a resident of Vermont, regardless of where they live now, and received an honorable discharge may be eligible for a state medal honoring their service. There are two medals: The Vermont Veteran's Medal (Bronze) and the Vermont Distinguished Service Medal (Silver). The Vermont Distinguished Service Medal is awarded to those who served in a combat theater. Veterans may choose to have the medals mailed to them or presented in a ceremony. In cases where the veteran is deceased, the medals may be requested by a family member. Medals are usually mailed within 4 weeks of our office receiving an application; those who request a ceremony may have to wait up to a year before there will be a presentations.

Virginia State Veteran's Benefits

The state of Virginia provides several veteran benefits. This section offers a brief description of each of the following benefits.

- Veteran Long Term Care Benefits
- Veteran Employment Benefits
- Veteran Education Benefits
- Other State Sponsored Veteran Benefits

Virginia Veteran Long Term Care

Virginia Veterans Care Center
The Virginia Veterans Care Center (VVCC) is a state-of-the-art model for long term health care and the only state home for veterans in the Commonwealth of Virginia.

The mission of the VVCC is to provide affordable, high quality, comprehensive nursing and domiciliary care to Commonwealth of Virginia residents who are admitted to the VVCC, are aged or infirm, and are honorably discharged veterans of the United States Armed Forces.

Virginia Veterans Care Center has 240 beds in the facility to provide comprehensive, high quality care with on-site laboratory work, x-rays, dental clinic, physical therapy, respiratory therapy, podiatry care, and many other ancillary health care services. The Salem VA Medical Center is also located next door for additional services for those qualified.

Additionally, the building and grounds offer an array of amenities to include wheelchair accessible nature trails and deck, library, chapel, barber shop, billiard room, wood working shop, and convenience store. The facility is nestled in the landscape of the Blue Ridge mountainside and has been enjoyed by our veterans since it was opened on Veterans Day, 1992.

Virginia Veteran Employment Programs

Virginia Employment Commission (VEC)
VEC provides job referral and placement resources available to assist veterans in finding jobs. Veterans Employment Representatives (LVERs) and Disabled Veterans Outreach

Program (DVOP) staff are available in most VEC offices to assist veterans with employment services.

Education Assistance Programs

Virginia Military Survivors and Dependents Education Program
The Military Survivors and Dependents Program (MSDEP) provides educations benefits to spouses and children of military service members killed, missing in action, taken prisoner, or who became at least 90 percent disabled as a result of military service in an armed conflict. Military service includes service in the United States Armed Forces, United States Armed Forces Reserves, the Virginia National Guard, or the Virginia National Guard Reserves. Armed conflict includes military operations against terrorism or as the result of a terrorist act, a peace-keeping mission, or any armed conflict after December 6, 1941. This program may pay for tuition of fee at any state-supported college or university in Virginia. Benefits are available for up to four years.

Honorary Diplomas for World War II Veterans
Veteran Honorary High School Diplomas recognize the life experiences of veterans who were unable to complete their high school education because of service n the armed forces during World War II, the Korean War, and the Vietnam War. Since the first honorary diplomas were issues in 2001, more than 1,000 have been awarded to veterans of these three wars.

To obtain an honorary diploma, a veteran may submit a statement to the Veterans Education Unit of the Virginia Department of Education describing his or her serve, The location of the last school attended, and affirming that he or she was unable to complete high school upon return to civilian life The guidelines also allow family members and veterans' organizations to submit this information on behalf of the veteran.

Other Virginia State Veteran Benefits

License Plates
The Virginia Department of Motor Vehicles (DMV) offers a variety of veteran and military-related license plates.

Lifetime Hunting and Fishing Licenses
The Virginia Department of Game and Inland Fisheries (VDGIF) offers a lifetime hunting and fishing license to service-connected, totally and permanently disabled veterans for minimal fee.

Washington State Veteran's Benefits

The state of Washington provides several veteran benefits. This section offers a brief description of each of the following benefits.

- Veteran Housing Benefits
- Veteran Financial Assistance Benefits
- Other State Sponsored Veteran Benefits

Washington Veteran Housing Programs

Homeless Veterans Program
WDVA provides outreach services for homeless veterans in Puget Sound. These services are designed to assist homeless veterans to become employable and reintegrated back into the labor market. Services include needs assessments, enrollments in appropriate programs, shelter and transitional housing placements, employment and training support services.

Eligible homeless veterans are provided with case management services and financial support to meet the needs of housing, transportation, food and clothing. The primary strategy for WDVA homeless veterans services is to promote job readiness development to improve homeless veterans competitiveness in the employment market.

Homeless Veterans Reintegration Project (HVRP)
The HVRP offers a structured, individually designed case management plan to make veterans employable and secure by providing, housing, food, transportation, living stability and employment support services.

State Veterans Homes
The Washington Veterans Home at Retsil, the Washington Soldiers Home and Colony near Orting, provide high-quality, long-term nursing and assisted-living care for honorably discharged veterans. The newly opened Spokane Veterans Home serves 100 residents needing long-term nursing care. All homes are Title 19 (Medicaid) certified.

Residents at each home receive comprehensive, no-cost medical benefits, prescription drug benefits and 24-hour nursing care.

Licensed medical staff, including registered nurses (RN), licensed practical nurses (LPN) and certified nursing assistants (CNA) provide personal care specifically tailored to each individual.

Washington Financial Assistance Programs

Veterans Estate Management Program
The Washington State Department of Veterans Affairs (WDVA) Veterans Estate Management Program offers protective payee services for veterans and family members who are incapable of managing their own financial affairs. By assuming custody of the individual's finances, the department ensures basic needs -- such as housing, food, clothing and medical care are provided.

The WDVA director is authorized to provide protective financial services to veterans and beneficiaries deemed in need of assistance. These services may include the following:

- Fiduciary appointment by the U.S. Department of Veterans Affairs;
- Representative payee appointment by the Social Security Administration; or
- Act as an executor of a veteran's estate.

PTSD Counseling Services

The Post Traumatic Stress Disorder (PTSD) Program attempts to create community-based avenues to counseling service that are less formal in nature, offering the highest level of confidentially possible. Services provided throughout the program include individual, couples, family, and veteran group counseling. Some contractors offer group services to women veterans and spouses of veterans. Veterans may be referred to specialized inpatient or outpatient treatment offered by the U.S. Department of Veterans Affairs Medical Centers or Vet Centers within Washington State.

Washington State offers several other benefits including special license plates, returning veterans transition assistance, reduced public transportation fees, reduced fee hunting and fishing licenses, and more.

West Virginia State Veteran's Benefits

The state of West Virginia provides several veteran benefits. This section offers a brief description of each of the following benefits.

- Veteran Housing Benefits
- Veteran Financial Assistance Benefits
- Veteran Employment Benefits
- Veteran Education Benefits
- Other State Veteran Benefits

West Virginia Veteran Housing Programs

Homestead Exemption for Certain Eligible Veterans
Specific information is available through the local County Assessor's Office.

State Veterans Home
Domiciliary care in Veterans Home is for ambulatory veterans who are able to go to the dining room without help; can dress themselves; can make their own beds, and can participate in an assigned therapeutic activity.

A veteran may be charged for care if he is able to pay.

West Virginia Financial Assistance Programs

Veterans Bonus
The West Virginia State Legislature approved four separate bonus programs for payment to veterans of World War I and World War II, Korean Conflict, the Vietnam Era and veterans of conflicts in Lebanon, Panama, Granada, and Desert Storm. The deadline for making application for these bonus programs has expired as indicated: World War I and World War II -- December 31, 1955; Korean Conflict -- June 30, 1959; Vietnam Era -- December 31, 1976;

Lebanon, Panama, Granada and Desert Storm -- June 30, 1994.

West Virginia Veteran Employment Programs

Veterans Preference
Under the West Virginia Civil Service System all veterans who have served under honorable conditions in the armed forces of the United States during World War II, Korea Conflict, Vietnam Era or during hostile conflict shall have five (5) points added to a final passing score. An additional five (5) points are added to a veteran's score if in receipt of the Purple Heart or has a compensable service-connected disability.

West Virginia Education Assistance Programs

State War Orphans Education
Provides for a waiver of tuition and registration fees in a state supported college or university for children between the ages of sixteen and twenty-three whose veteran parent served in World War I, World War II, Korean Conflict, Vietnam Era or any time of conflict as declared by Congress. Parent must have died in such wartime period, or, if subsequent to discharge, death must have been the result of disability incurred in such wartime service.

Veterans Re-Education Act Fund
The West Virginia Legislature provides tuition assistance to those veterans who need a new vocation due to dislocation or unemployment. Veteran must have exhausted the G. I. Bill and be in need of tuition assistance.

Other West Virginia State Veteran Benefits

Agent Orange Program
The program administered by the West Virginia Division of Health expired July 1, 1989. However, assistance is provided to Korean and Vietnam veterans exposed to certain chemicals, defoliants or herbicides or other causative agents, including Agent Orange from the US Department of Veterans Affairs, Medicine and Surgery.

Free License -- Automobile
Provides special vehicle license plates, DV Tags without fee to any veteran in receipt of an auto grant or who is permanently and totally disabled due to service-connected causes, and former POW Tag as certified by the US Department of Veterans Affairs. Also recent legislation provides for Purple Heart Tags for those wounded in action and Pearl Harbor Survivors Tags for West Virginia veterans who were at Pearl Harbor during the attack on December 7, 1941. Veteran Plate for honorably discharged veterans for a one-time fee of $10.00 over and above the regular license fee required by Motor Vehicles.

Free Hunting and Fishing Privileges
For 100% service-connected veterans and those veterans in receipt of a VA auto grant.

Wisconsin State Veteran's Benefits

The state of Wisconsin provides several veteran benefits. This section offers a brief description of each of the following benefits.

- Property Tax Credit
- Veteran Employment Benefits
- Veteran Education Benefits
- Other State Veteran Benefits

Property Tax Credit

Wisconsin Veterans and Surviving Spouses Property Tax Credit
This credit program provides a refundable property tax credit for the primary residence (in-state) via the state income tax form for:

- Eligible veterans age 65 or older who entered service from Wisconsin and have a combined VA service-connected disability rating of 100%.
- The unremarried surviving spouse of an eligible veteran.
- The unremarried surviving spouse of a veteran who entered active duty as a Wisconsin resident, died in the line of duty, and was a Wisconsin resident at the time of death.

Wisconsin Veteran Employment Programs

Transition Assistance for Veterans Leaving Active Duty
Veterans transitioning from active duty can contact the WDVA Transition & Employment Section for state-wide employment information. The office provides employment assistance and labor market information to veterans in transition from active duty to civilian life and the civilian job market in Wisconsin.

Local Veterans Employment Representatives
Employment assistance is available to all Wisconsin veterans in the local one-stop job centers. Veterans Employment Representatives complement the information provided at a Department of Defense Transition Assistance Program (TAP) Seminar.

Veterans as Apprentices
Veterans, their eligible dependents, eligible members of the National Guard, and the Reserves may benefit from Apprenticeship programs.

For more information on apprenticeship opportunities in Wisconsin, visit the Bureau of Apprenticeship Standards.

Hire Veterans First
The Hire Veterans First program is a National initiative established by the Veterans' Employment and Training Service (VETS) of the Department of Labor (DOL). Their objective is to show support for America's veterans to send the message out to employers "Hire a Veteran First -- American Excellence at Work".

Veterans Preference

Civil Service Preferences (State) --- Eligible veterans are entitled to an extra 10 points added to a passing score on a state civil service examination. Veterans with a VA approved SCD of less than 30 percent are entitled to 15 points and those with a rating of 30 percent or more are entitled to 20 points added to their passing score. Spouses of certain disabled or deceased eligible veterans may also have points added to a passing score. (Preference points are available only when you initially apply for permanent state employment.)

Veterans with a 30 percent or greater SCD may be hired for a permanent, entry-level position with the State of Wisconsin on a noncompetitive basis. Check with the hiring agency for more information.

Employment Assistance Opportunities

- Entrepreneurial Training --- a partnership between the Wisconsin Department of Veterans Affairs (WDVA) and the Veterans Corporation offers Wisconsin veterans starting a new business timely entrepreneurial training.

- Troops to Teachers Program --- helps Wisconsin veterans obtain alternative teaching certification so they can obtain employment as teachers and teachers' aides. The Wisconsin Department of Veterans Affairs (WDVA) operates a placement office for the program, which is funded by the Department of Defense.

- Unemployment Compensation for Ex-Servicemembers (UCX) --- Application for Unemployment Insurance, including UCX, is made by telephone:

- Veterans Business Training Center --- A program of the Military Order of the Purple Heart Service Foundation helping disabled veterans find employment. A 15 week 600 hour training program pays while learning, is accredited, and allows graduates to work in their home.

- Vocational Rehabilitation --- This benefit may be available through either the VA or the Wisconsin Department of Workforce Development, Division of Vocational Rehabilitation. Your County Veterans Service Officer or Veterans Representative will advise you concerning eligibility for the VA benefit.

- Wisconsin Women's Business Initiative --- Learn about an economic development corporation that provides quality business education, technical assistance and access to capital for small businesses throughout Wisconsin.

Wisconsin Veteran Education and Training

Wisconsin G.I. Bill for Dependents
A 100% remission is provided to the qualifying dependents of an eligible veteran:

- Spouse; or
- Unremarried Surviving Spouse; or
- Child between the ages of 18 and 25,

Wisconsin G.I. Bill for Veterans
Qualifying veterans receive a 50% remission (Effective Fall Semester 2005). In accordance

with 2005 Wisconsin Act 468, effective Fall Semester 2007, the remission will increase to a full 100%.

Veterans Education (VetEd) Reimbursement Grant

The Veterans Education (VetEd) grant program provides a reimbursement grant based on a credit-bank system that is based on length of active duty military service to eligible veterans who have not yet been awarded a bachelor's degree for the reimbursement of tuition and fees following successful course completion at an eligible UW, technical college, or approved private institution of higher learning.

Veterans may concurrently receive Chapter 30 Montgomery G.I. Bill (VA) benefits and VetEd for the same semester. However, individuals eligible for Wisconsin G.I. Bill benefits must apply for, and use those benefits in order to be eligible for VetEd reimbursement. VetEd reimbursement will be reduced to the extent that tuition and fees have already been paid by other grants, scholarships, and remissions provided for the payment of tuition and fees.

Entrepreneurial Training

WDVA, in cooperation with The Veterans Corporation, has offered FastTrac Planning and FastTrac NewVenture entrepreneurial training courses. The Veterans Corporation is no longer continuing this program. WDVA is currently working with additional partners to provide entrepreneurial training to Wisconsin veterans.

'If you are a veteran interested in entrepreneurial training or services to assist you in starting, managing or improving your business, please consider contacting one or more of these organizations.

Tuition Residency for Wisconsin Veterans

Under state law, veterans who entered active duty as a Wisconsin resident retain permanent eligibility for in-state tuition at University of Wisconsin System institutions. To be eligible, a person who was a resident of Wisconsin at the time of entry into federal active duty military service, who is a resident of and living in this state at the time of registering at a UW institution, and who meets the criteria for determination of veteran status under s. 45.01(12) of the Wisconsin Statutes are eligible for in-state tuition rates at UW institutions. There are no restrictions regarding residency after entry onto active duty but before registering at the UW institution under the program.

Academic Credit for Military Experience (ACME)

The ACME program is designed for active military personnel and veterans to create and maintain a transcript of their military experience. Use the transcript and the ACME system to determine possible equivalency credit at Wisconsin Colleges, Technical Colleges, and Universities.

Visit the Wisconsin Dept.of Veterans Affairs website for contact information and benefits assistance.

Job Retraining Grants

Recently unemployed or underemployed veterans may receive up to $3,000 per year, for a maximum of two years, if they have a financial need while being retrained for employment..

Troops to Teachers (TTT)

Troops to Teachers (TTT) is a joint program of the U.S. Departments of Defense and Education that assists departing active duty military personnel, veterans and certain members/retirees who are associated with the reserve components, to transition to new careers as public school teachers.

Other Wisconsin State Veteran Benefits

Hunting & Fishing Licenses for Wisconsin Veterans
Wisconsin disabled veterans with a combined service-connected disability rating by the U.S. Department of Veterans Affairs (VA) of 70% or greater are eligible for a disabled veteran reduced-fee fishing license. The fishing license must be renewed annually, and does not exempt the holder from the need to purchase required fishing stamps. When purchasing the license at a DNR or County Clerk's office, the applicant must provide a copy of a letter from the VA that indicates receipt of VA disability benefits and specifies the percentage of disability.

Military Funeral Honors Program
The Military Funeral Honors Program (MFHP) in Wisconsin provides a final tribute to the men and women who served our state and nation honorably as members of the U.S. armed forces.

Wisconsin Veterans Memorial Cemeteries
Upon meeting eligibility standards, veterans are provided a burial at no cost, spouses and dependent children will incur a burial fee.

Transportation to VA Medical Appointments
Wisconsin veterans may use one of two programs that assist veterans who need help getting to VA medical appointments. The Wisconsin Department of the Disabled American Veterans operates several vans around the state that normally stop at predetermined locations and then transport to the various medical centers. For veterans who live in locations not served by the DAV most counties provide some type of assistance.

Veterans & Military License Plates
Special license plates are available to veterans, retired military service members, medal recipients, and members of the active or reserve military.

Driver Licensing, & Vehicle Registration
When the U.S. is involved in a military conflict, anyone who is a member of the military and stationed outside of Wisconsin is considered to be on "active duty" for the purposes of eligibility for modified procedures for the following driver licensing and registration measures: Driver license renewal; duplicate driver license; insurance information; suspended or revoked license reinstatement; medical report; vehicle registration renewal; dealer and salesperson licenses; motor carrier fees and reports; and special license plates.

Wyoming State Veteran's Benefits

The state of Wyoming provides several veteran benefits. This section offers a brief description of each of the following benefits.

- Veteran Housing Benefits
- Veteran Financial Assistance Benefits

- Veteran Employment Benefits
- Veteran Education Benefits
- Other State Veteran Benefits

Wyoming Veteran Housing Programs

Veterans' Home of Wyoming
This home is located on the historic site of Fort McKinney. It was built in the summer and fall of 1878. The home was established in 1895 with the first member being housed at Fort D. A. Russell (now F.E. Warren AFB) in Cheyenne, Wyoming. The home and its resident were transferred from Cheyenne to the home's present location in 1903. It is located three miles west of Buffalo, one-half mile south of Highway 16, at the base of the majestic Big Horn Mountains. Clear Creek from the Big Horns runs through the center of the area surrounding the home and supplies the fresh water for the resident trout pond.

Eligibility

- Honorably discharged Veteran and resident of Wyoming
- Cannot be gainfully employed
- Allowed to have some qualified non-Veterans
    - Must be related to a Veteran that would be eligible
    - Non-Veteran admitted when there is a 10% vacancy

For more information, please visit the Veteran's Home of Wyoming website or call (307) 684-5511.

For more information contact the Wyoming Veterans Commission:

Wyoming Veterans Commission
5410 Bishop Blvd.
Cheyenne, WY 82009
(307) 777-8152
(307) 777-8150 fax
larry.barttelbort@wyo.gov

Wyoming Financial Assistance Programs

Wyoming Veterans Tax Exemption
The exemption applies to taxes on a Veteran's primary residence lowering the assessed value by $3,000. The $800 cap was removed in 2007. Veterans who reached the previous cap should reapply. Veterans should check with their County Assessor each year prior to the deadline as the reapplication process may vary.

Veterans must be residents of Wyoming three or more years prior to claiming the tax exemption and must have a DD 214 or equivalent from their branch of service. Additionally, one of the following must apply:

- Served in the Armed Forces during one of the following periods:
  World War II December 7, 1941 - December 31, 1946

Korean War June 27, 1950 - January 31, 1955
Vietnam War February 28, 1961 - May 7, 1975
OR

- Must have served overseas during an armed conflict and received an Armed Forces Expeditionary Medal or equivalent.
OR

- Be a disabled Veteran with a compensable service connected disability as certified by the U.S. Department of Veterans Affairs or a branch of the Armed Forces of the United States. VA or DOD agency disability letter required.

- Be the surviving spouse of a qualifying Veteran who resides in Wyoming and does not remarry.

Family Support Grant Program
Wyoming Guard, Reserves and Active personnel have available a newly created trust fund administered by the Adjutant General from which "grantor of last resort" funds are available for service members and their family members in need of assistance.

Wyoming Veteran Employment Programs

Wyoming Department of Workforce Services
The Department of Workforce Services (DWS) is Wyoming's newest state agency, dedicated to developing a demand-driven workforce that is responsive to Wyoming's businesses, citizens, and economy. Veterans Services ensure assistance is provided or targeted to veterans, including services for veterans who are disabled or have employment issues. A variety of employment and training services are available through DWS and can be easily accessed at: www.wyomingworkforce.org

Employment Assistance

The Wyoming Military Department also has a program to help traditional Guard members and their family members find civilian employment opportunities within their communities. The Wyoming National Guard Jobs Coordinator can assist with resume writing, job interview skills and other tips. Contact the coordinator at (307) 772-5942.

Wyoming Education Assistance Programs

Free tuition and fees for education of War Orphans and Veterans

10 semesters of free tuition and fees at UW or Community Colleges for those who meet the following eligibility requirements:

- Resident of Wyoming for at least 1 year before application

- Discharge other than dishonorable

- Vietnam Veteran from August 5, 1964 to May 7, 1975

- Overseas combat Veteran who received an Expeditionary Medal or equivalent

- Surviving Spouse or dependent of an eligible Veteran who died in active service

(Dependent must be 22 years of age or less at time of application)

To apply bring your DD-214 to the educational institution's financial aid office - Wyoming Veteran's Education Consultant - Phil O'Connor (307) 772-5053

Wyoming National Guard 100% State Educational Assistance Plan
The 100% State Educational Assistance Plan is for Wyoming National Guard members that want to pursue higher education. The plan pays 100% of the tuition and mandatory fees at Wyoming Junior colleges and at the University of Wyoming. The plan pays a determined amount each year for those private schools in Wyoming that are VA approved.

Guard members can use the state educational assistance to complete one degree or certificate program. This includes: Certificates, Associate, Bachelors, Masters, or PhD program. The combination of Certificate, Associate to Bachelor counts as one degree.

Members can use the GI Bill and kicker if qualified with the 100% State Educational Assistance Plan.

Education Benefits For National Guard Family Members: Matriculation fees and tuition paid in the University of Wyoming or any junior college or vocational training institution in Wyoming for child or spouse of Wyoming National Guard member who dies or sustains permanent total disability from duty as guardsman while on state active duty or any authorized training duty.

Operation Recognition (High School Diploma)
Any Veteran of WWII, Korea, or Vietnam who was not able to complete their high school education prior to entering the service may be eligible to receive their diplomas. Diplomas can also be awarded posthumously.
Call 1-800-833-5987 or (307) 265-7372 for application.

For more information contact the Wyoming Veterans Commision:

Wyoming Veterans Commission
5410 Bishop Blvd.
Cheyenne, WY 82009
(307) 777-8152
(307) 777-8150 fax
larry.barttelbort@wyo.gov

Other Wyoming State Veteran Benefits

Oregon Trail State Veterans' Cemetery
The Oregon Trail State Veterans' Cemetery has been established through the cooperative efforts of the Veterans' Commission acting for the State of Wyoming and the National Cemetery Administration of the U. S. Department of Veterans Affairs, successor to the Veterans Administration. The Wyoming Military Department supervises and controls the state veterans' cemetery.

Every veteran that received any discharge, other than dishonorable, from the Armed Forces of the United States is eligible for burial in the cemetery. The spouse, handicapped or minor child of an eligible veteran may also qualify for burial in the State Veterans' Cemetery, providing that the interment of the qualifying family member is in the same burial plot as that provided for the veteran.

Apply through the local funeral home or call (307) 236-6673

Payment for Burial Details
Payment of $50 for services. All VSO funeral details that have pre-registered with the WVC are eligible.

The Board of County Commissioners will provide for the preparation of and transmittal to and burial in the Veteran's cemetery of any other than a dishonorably discharged Veteran who dies leaving insufficient funds for funeral expenses. The amount expended is not to exceed $500.00.

Call 1-800-833-5987 or (307) 265-7372 for more information and application.

Burial of Indigent Veterans
Counties are obliged to provide up to $500 for the burial of indigent veterans upon proof that the deceased veteran received a discharge other than dishonorable for service on behalf of the United States in World War II, or any preceding war, or the Korean or Vietnam wars. The indigent veteran must have died in the county paying the expenses and proof must be shown that he/she left insufficient means to defray the expense.

Veterans' Guardianships
The Uniform Veterans' Guardianship Act has been adopted in Wyoming and governs the handling of guardianship estates of wards that are beneficiaries under the laws administered by the U. S. Department of Veterans Affairs (VA). The VA is a party in interest in any proceeding brought under this Act. Guardians can have no more than five wards, and regular accountings must be made.

Free (Confidential) Recording of Honorable Discharges
Wyoming law grants all veterans who receive an honorable discharge from the military services of the United States the right of having his/her discharge papers, usually the DD 214 or the Honorable Discharge certificate bearing the DD 214 information on its reverse side, recorded free in the office of the county clerk if the documents have not been recorded previously in another county of the state. The County Clerk keeps this document confidential.

Special Veterans License Plates
The vehicle must be titled in the name of the Veteran or may have joint ownership with a member of the immediate family. Apply directly to the County Treasurer at least 60 days before registration of the vehicle expires. All special license plates are issued once in an eight year period and must be renewed annually at the County Treasurer's Office. All applicants for special license plates must be Wyoming residents and meet the eligibility criteria as prescribed by Wyoming statute. Application, registration, and plate costs can be obtained from the local County Treasurer's Office.

- Prisoner of War (POW) License Plate - first plate is FREE, additional plates may be purchased

- Purple Heart Recipient (PH) License Plate - must be purchased

- Disabled Veteran (DV) License Plate - One FREE set of plates for Veterans at least 50% VA disabled, no additional plates may be purchased

- Pearl Harbor Survivor (PHS) License Plate - must be purchased
- National Guard (NG) License Plate - must be purchased

Wyoming Veteran License Plate Stickers - License plate stickers that represent various periods of service are available for purchase from the Wyoming Veterans Commission. Stickers cost $11.50 for auto and trucks and $11.00 for motorcycles. Only one set may be displayed on any one vehicle, no trailers. Stickers previously purchased by the Veteran may also be purchased by surviving spouses. Proceeds go to the Wyoming Veterans Commission Trust Fund. For more information and to request applications, call (800) 833-5987.

Wyoming Veteran License Plate Stickers Available application.

Free Veterans Game and Fish Licenses
The Wyoming Game and Fish Department offers a number of hunting and fishing licenses to qualified Veterans. Applicants must provide a letter from the VBA Regional Office certifying eligibility. Call (800) 842-1934 for application information or visit one of the Department Regional Offices located in Casper, Cody, Green River, Jackson, Lander, Laramie, Pinedale or Sheridan.

Free Fishing License 50% Disabled Veteran, resident of Wyoming for not less than one year and submit a letter from the VBA Regional Office certifying the 50% level of service connected disability of the applicant.

Free Bird, Small Game, and Fishing Licenses 100% Disabled Veteran, resident of Wyoming for not less than one year and submit a letter from the VBA Regional Office certifying the 100% level of service connected disability of the applicant.

Free Hunting and Fishing Licenses While on Leave Any Wyoming resident who is on active duty in the U.S. Military deployed to a combat zone, who is home on leave.

Special Limited Fishing Permit for Hospitalized Veterans In coordination with the Wyoming Game and Fish Department, a free license can be issued by any VA Hospital within Wyoming, Wyoming Department of Health or Wyoming Department of Family Services. Veteran must fish under the direct control of the institution.

Pioneer Veteran Bird, Small Game, and Fishing License For any Wyoming Veteran who is 65 or older and has lived in Wyoming for 30 or more continuous years.

Free State Parks Pass Wyoming State Parks & Cultural Resources offers a 50% Disabled Veteran Annual Day Use and Camping Lifetime Permit. You must be a resident of Wyoming for not less than one year and submit a letter from the VBA Regional Office certifying the 50% level of service connected disability of the applicant. For more information, call 307-777-6303.

County Veteran Service Officer(s)
A new program that is in its early stages is the County Veteran Service Officer (CVSO) program. These are dedicated and trained volunteers that can help a veteran start the process of accessing State and Federal benefits. At the present time, Wyoming has only two southwestern counties participating in the CVSO program, but in surrounding states, there are literally hundreds of CVSOs that help their state veterans access benefits.

Wyoming's Veterans' Memorial Museum
Wyoming's Veterans' Memorial Museum was dedicated Memorial Day 2002 thereby making it

the first state veterans' memorial honoring all veterans of all services of all wars. It accepts and displays donated war related memorabilia and artifacts, and it collects recordings and printed copy of veterans' experiences for history research scholars as well as books and other publications.

Wyoming Veterans' Commission

The Commission is an agency created by state law in 1975 that is part of the Wyoming Military Department headed by the Adjutant General. It keeps informed on issues affecting Wyoming veterans and makes appropriate recommendations to the Governor and legislature. By statute, the Commission's duties include:

- Study all federal and state legislation affection veterans, their spouses, dependents and beneficiaries;

- Establish liaison with agencies dealing with veteran's affairs;

- Make recommendations to the legislature and to the governor concerning veterans; and

- Adopt policies and procedures necessary to administer then veterans' burial team account pursuant to W.S. 19-14-109.

For more information contact the Wyoming Veterans Commission:

Wyoming Veterans Commission
5410 Bishop Blvd.
Cheyenne, WY 82009
(307) 777-8152
(307) 777-8150 fax
larry.barttelbort@wyo.gov

Important Cases to Know About

The following are excerpts from cases that have been adjudicated over the years, and sections of pertinent code. This list is by no means complete, but look through it and see if there is anything that applies to your situation.

38 U.S.C.A. § 5107 (West 2002); 38 C.F.R. § 3.102 (2009)

When there is an approximate balance of evidence regarding the merits of an issue material to the determination of the matter, the benefit of the doubt in resolving each such issue shall be given to the claimant.

Gilbert v. Derwinski, 1 Vet. App. 49, 53 (1990)

The United States Court of Appeals for Veterans Claims (the Court) stated that "a veteran need only demonstrate that there is an 'approximate balance of positive and negative evidence' in order to prevail."

38 U.S.C.A. § 5103A (West 2002); 38 C.F.R. § 3.159 (2009)

In general, the VCAA provides that VA shall make reasonable efforts to assist a claimant in obtaining evidence necessary to substantiate claims for VA benefits, unless no reasonable possibility exists that such assistance would aid in substantiating the claims. The law provides that the assistance provided by VA shall include providing a medical examination or obtaining a medical opinion when such an examination or opinion is necessary to make a decision on the claims. An examination is deemed "necessary" if the record does not contain sufficient medical evidence for VA to make a decision on the claims.

Coburn v. Nicholson, 19 Vet. App. 427 (2006).

A medical opinion cannot be disregarded solely on the rationale that the medical opinion is based on a history provided by the veteran.

Jandreau v. Nicholson, 492 F.3d 1372, 1377 (Fed. Cir. 2007)

Depending on the evidence and contentions of record in a particular case, lay evidence can be competent and sufficient to establish a diagnosis of a condition.

38 C.F.R. § 3.159(a)(2); see also Layno v. Brown, 6 Vet. App. 471 (1994).

Lay persons are competent to provide evidence regarding things they have personally observed, including symptoms that are capable of lay observation and when those symptoms occurred.

Buchanan v. Nicholson, 451 F.3d 1331, 1137 (Fed. Cir. 2006)

The Board cannot determine that lay evidence lacks credibility merely because it is unaccompanied by contemporaneous medical evidence.

Clemons v. Shinseki, 23 Vet. App. 1 (2009)

The Board notes that the Veteran's claim constituted a claim for service connection for an acquired psychiatric disability, however diagnosed. As such, the claim must be considered a claim for service connection for any and all psychiatric disabilities clinically indicated.

DON'T LET THEM TELL YOU THAT IF YOU DON'T HAVE ALL THE SYMPTOMS YOU GET THE NEXT LOWEST RATING!!!!!!!!!!!!!!!!!!!!

"The Board is aware that the Veteran does not have all of the symptoms listed in the criteria for a 50 percent rating - namely, circumstantial, circumlocutory or stereotyped speech; panic attacks more than once a week; difficulty in understanding complex commands; and impaired judgment. See 38 C.F.R. § 4.130. The Veteran is not required to prove the presence of all, most, or even some, of the enumerated symptoms recited under the rating criteria. The use of the term "such as" in the general rating formula for mental disorders in 38 C.F.R. § 4.130 demonstrates that the symptoms after that phrase are not intended to constitute an exhaustive list, but rather are to serve as examples of the type and degree of symptoms, or their effects, that would justify a particular rating." See Mauerhan v. Principi, 16 Vet. App. 436, 442 (2002).

Resources

Here is a list of resources for your use.

Directory of Veteran's Service Organizations - http://www1.va.gov/vso/index.cfm?template=view&SortCategory=4

Hadit.com – A community of veterans - http://www.hadit.com/

Department of Veteran's Affairs Forms - http://www4.va.gov/vaforms/

The Wounded Warrior Project - https://www.woundedwarriorproject.org/

US Veterans Resource - http://www.vetsresource.com/

Quintesential Careers (Job source for Vets) - http://www.quintcareers.com/former_military.html

Daily Strenght – Free Veteran's Resources - http://www.dailystrength.org/health_blogs/teamds/article/free-resources-and-services-for-armed-forces-veterans

Lawyers Serving Veterans - http://www.lawyersservingwarriors.com/resources.html

Camp Patriot – Outdoors Activities for Disabled Vets - http://www.camppatriot.org/aboutus.html

Veteran's Support Center – Lots of Information on this Site - http://veteransupportcenter.org/?

_kk=veteran&_kt=4b709d18-c8bf-4ad5-b27e-445c8c056f01

National Veteran's Foundation - http://nvf.org/

Directory of United States Governors, Senators, and Representatives - http://directory.usayfoundation.org/

Unclassified document on the Air Defence Project CHECO may show that Agent Orange was used on US Bases in Thailand during Vietnam. That document can be reached at

http://www.afhra.af.mil/shared/media/document/AFD-080819-065.pdf

www.ingramcontent.com/pod-product-compliance
Lightning Source LLC
Chambersburg PA
CBHW071357310526
45789CB00020B/407